VOGUE & BUTTERICK'S
DESIGNER SEWING
TECHNIQUES

VOGUE & BUTTERICK'S
DESIGNER SEWING TECHNIQUES

Introduction by Nancy Fleming

A FIRESIDE BOOK
Published by SIMON & SCHUSTER INC.
New York London Toronto Sydney Tokyo Singapore

FIRESIDE
SIMON & SCHUSTER, INC.
Rockefeller Center
1230 Avenue of the Americas
New York, New York 10020

Senior Editor Linda Lee, The Sewing Workshop, San Francisco
Editor Kit Schlich
Production Editor Rosalie Cooke
Contributing Writers Dort Johnson, Barbara Kelly, Marcy Tilton
Associate Contributors Laura Hotchkiss Brown, Candice Bushell, Caroline E. Kelly, Kathy McBride, Lysa Schloesser
Editorial Assistants Stephanie Hoferer, Darchelle Woltkamp

President and Chief Executive Officer John E. Lehmann
Publisher Art Joinnides
Senior Vice President, Editorial Director Patricia Perry
Vice President, Creative Director Sidney Escowitz
Fashion Director Cindy Rose
Technical Director Janet DuBane
Art Directors/Cover Design Jeffrey Engel, Joe Vior
Production Manager Caroline Testaverde-Politi
Technical Consultant Joanne Pugh-Gannon
Marketing Consultant Mike Shatzkin

Book development, design and production provided by BMR, Corte Madera, CA
Publishing Director Jack Jennings
Project Manager Jo Lynn Taylor
Electronic Page Layout Donna Yuen

Printed in the U.S.A. by R.R. Donnelly
10 9 8 7 6 5 4 3 2 1
Library of Congress Cataloging in Publication Data
Vogue & Butterick's Designer Sewing Techniques/Introduction by Nancy Fleming.
p.   cm.
"Fireside book." Includes index.
ISBN: 0-671-88878-1
1. Sewing.   2. Clothing and dress.
I. Vogue & Butterick Patterns.   II. Title: Vogue & Butterick's Designer Sewing Techniques.
TT705.V66 1994   94-1210
648.4'04–dc20   CIP

To Our Readers

Dear Reader,

Home sewers have many bonds, but perhaps the strongest is our desire for creativity. As a school girl, I made my clothes out of necessity, since my allowance and taste in fashionable trends were not a good match. Soon I discovered the pride we all feel when responding to a compliment with the phrase, "Thank you, I made it myself!" Not only could I duplicate the looks I saw in fashion magazines, I could also individualize my wardrobe by choosing fabrics, colors, and accessories that worked best for me.

Sewing changed my life dramatically when I won the Miss America title using sewing for my talent presentation. The last line in my commentary was, "Have basic dress, will travel." This sign-off turned out to be extremely prophetic!

Through the years, my interest and skill in sewing have remained a way to express myself, whether sewing for my family, my television career wardrobe, my home, or crafts for gifts or charity bazaars.

The television series *Sewing Today* allows me an opportunity to combine many years of experience as a television show host and a home sewer. It is an exciting chance to meet the world's top designers in fashion, home decorating, and crafts. We hope to inspire you with the very best in contemporary design. Through the series and this book we also intend to increase sewing expertise with sewing information that utilizes professional techniques and the marvelous technology available today for home use. It's great fun for me to continue to learn more about something that has brought so much pleasure into my life, and it is an added joy to be able to share this creative process with you.

Happy Sewing,

Nancy Fleming

Contents

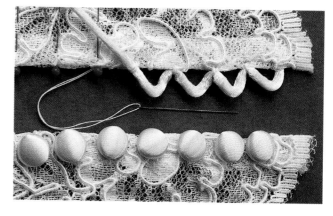

Donna Karan

DKNY

Linda Allard for Ellen Tr

Bellville Sassoon

DKNY

Calvin Klein

CHAPTER 1

Contemporary Sewing

Creating your own designer wardrobe can be an exciting and rewarding adventure. Designers and pattern companies are ready to assist you on your quest and show you how to achieve professional-looking results.

As home sewing grows in popularity, so does the sophistication and savvy of the contemporary home sewer. She knows fabric, is familiar with designer labels, and longs to create the look of quality ready-to-wear. She is eager to duplicate the construction techniques that young designers learn in fashion schools behind the scenes-and at the great couturier houses of Europe and America.

Contemporary patterns offer the home sewer elegant fashions with the intricate detailing of designer couture. Pattern companies send their merchandisers and design directors to attend the collections in Europe and America and to purchase garments for pattern reproductions. *Designer Sewing Techniques* hopes to bring the sewer closer to these reproductions and the people who created them, and to the techniques used in giving them a professional look.

This book is geared editorially, visually and technically to high fashion sewing. It will lead you by the hand through many intricate sewing phases. It is a great challenge to create a garment from an exciting design which has been precisely translated into a pattern. Designer and technique are united for your inspiration and guidance in customized fit, style and technical information.

The Design Process

In most designer workrooms, the creative process begins with the development of a *croquis*—a simple but detailed sketch of the envisioned garment on a body. Some designers execute a preliminary draping with the proposed fabric on a dress form or model before drawing. The designer gives the final sketch to the draper, who then drapes a muslin on a dress form, creating a three-dimensional version of the designer's sketch. This three-dimensional beginning is what gives designer garments their fabulous shape and fit.

Once the designer approves the muslin, it is marked, removed from the dress form, and made into a flat pattern. This pattern is then cut in the final fabrics; as many as five different fabrics may be used to explore the possibilities of the final garment. The draper and assistant designer then supervise a sample maker in the sewing of the garment.

Construction techniques are carefully chosen—from basting to finishing—to enhance the overall design of the garment.

From Designers to You

The development of a garment from concept through printed pattern is a fascinating story in itself. Here's what happens behind the scenes.

Creating a Pattern

A designer garment goes through many stages from designer original to home sewing pattern. First the garment, along with its flat pattern, goes to a pattern

A designer garment will be fitted many times to assure accuracy of fit, style and proportion. In these fittings, the details of the garment are painstakingly worked out. Once finished, this "sample" garment becomes the gorgeous creation we see on the runway, in the fashion magazines and in pattern catalogs.

maker who drapes a standard size 10 line-for-line copy of the garment, including all interfacings, linings, and details down to the last hook and eye. This muslin copy is compared with the original garment to make sure that all the design lines and details are identical. It's also evaluated to make sure that it's easily sewable by the home sewer.

A "master pattern block" is traced from this muslin and marked with all the construction symbols such as darts, seams, and notches. From this master pattern, a dressmaker constructs the garment using a home sewing machine and traditional dressmaking construction techniques. The pattern is then tested for its suitability for printed, striped, plaid, diagonal, and napped fabric, and any special types recommended by the designer. A fit model tries on the garment for a final inspection and assurance that the design in fact fits well and has appropriate ease.

Next, the master pattern block is graded—scaled up and down for all pattern sizes. The difference between sizes is based on standardized measurements and the style of the garment. The grading is done by a computer, which adds or subtracts a carefully predetermined amount to certain areas to achieve the different pattern sizes.

While the pattern pieces are measured for layout diagrams, a writer creates the sewing guide instructions and an illustrator executes the technical drawings. Photographs, sketches, yardage requirements, and fabric recommendations are gathered together for the pattern envelope. Everything is checked one last time before the pattern is manufactured. Once printed and distributed, it is ready for your selection.

In many ways, the designer's process parallels that of the home sewer who conceives an idea for a garment, chooses fabric and pattern, makes a muslin, and then cuts, sews, fits and finishes that garment. With all the research and development that goes into a designer pattern you should feel comfortable using it in the creation of your design.

Focusing On You

Creating a flattering image through the combination of fit, fabric and style is a challenging task. You need to train your eye to see yourself realistically before you are able to make judgments about the fabrics, patterns and styles that will work best for you.

Developing Fashion Sense

Begin your self-training process by reading information about design and image. Next, try on your own wardrobe in front of a full length mirror. Observe what shapes work best; take notes. Then visit a department store or boutique where you can try on a wide variety of tops, jackets, skirts, pants and dresses. Many people gravitate to the same style and colors because they find them comfortable and non-threatening. If you are unable to get a clear picture of yourself, hire someone who will point out colors, lines, textures and details that work for you.

This self-awareness is a never-ending process because life styles and bodies change; it is a lifelong quest that always holds surprises. Once you feel comfortable with your view of yourself, you need to see what the fashion world has put out there for your enjoyment. Each designer has a philosophy and seasonal statement for your interpretation.

Observe how designers are using fabrics and shapes together. Their combinations are the result of painstaking testing. What you see on the pages of magazines and in the stores is a good indication of the mix of fabric and patterns.

The jacket is a pivotal piece in a wardrobe. What is the overall shape? Does it cover the hips, nip in at the waist, button high or low? What is the collar like? The armholes, pockets and details? Last but not least, study the fabric: color, texture and weight. Note the finishing touches: buttons, braid, piping, etc. Look for similar details being repeated. Many ideas are not original, but refinements and restatements of previously successful designs. They appear around the world almost simultaneously because we now live in a global society.

After a while this kind of observing will become second nature to you. You will develop a greater ability to look through a pattern catalog and determine which patterns will work for you.

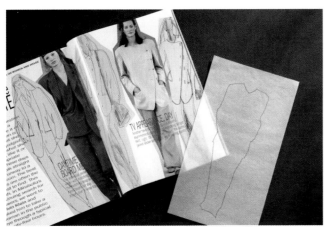

Draw the Silhouette
To develop an eye-to-brain connection for details, take a felt-tip pen and trace the outside lines of the photographed garments in fashion magazines. You can see the silhouette readily—long and lean, short and sassy, oversized...

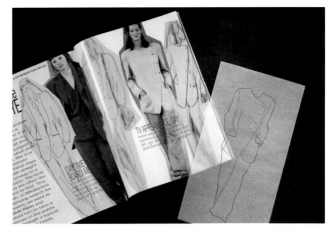

Draw the Design Lines
Using a pen of another color, trace the inside seamlines and darts of photographed garments to see if straight, curved or diagonal lines are emphasized. Trace around details such as collars and pockets to determine their proportion and shape.

Choosing a Pattern For You

As a means to assist you and offer insight into what looks are flattering on you, this system describes four basic figure shapes, and recommends flattering pattern styles for each. The success of your sewing endeavors lies in knowing your figure type well and working within its confines.

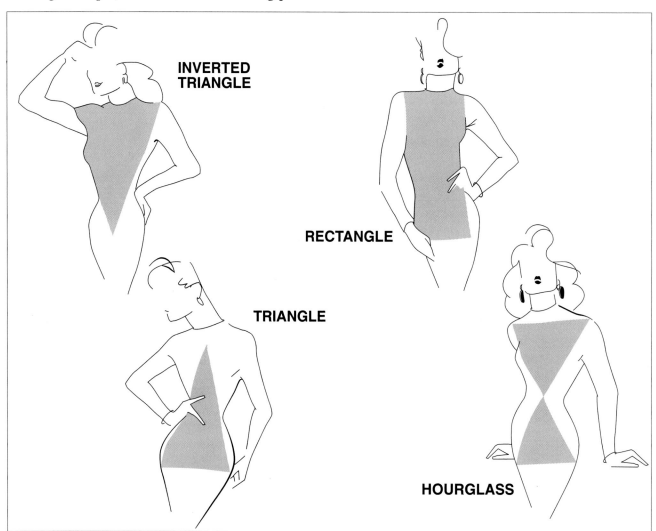

INVERTED TRIANGLE

RECTANGLE

TRIANGLE

HOURGLASS

THE FOUR FIGURE TYPES

You will probably fall into one of these categories:

The INVERTED TRIANGLE is top heavy and carries weight through the bust or shoulders. Minimize the large bust by selecting styles with an open-throat scooped neckline. If arms are fleshy, look for styles with deeper armholes and loose-fitting sleeves.

The TRIANGLE has a heavier bottom half that requires a balanced top emphasis. Wear shoulder pads and use care when selecting skirts and pants. Wear matte and dark-toned hosiery. Pants should be non-clingy and loose in the hip and thigh area.

The RECTANGLE figure is straight up and down, with little or no waist definition; the look is equally slender or equally full. Select styles that give the suggestion of a waistline. Use horizontal lines at the shoulder or hips to create the illusion of a waist. Select slightly shaped or full jackets that camouflage the lack of a waist.

The HOURGLASS is well-balanced and well-proportioned. The bust and hips are nearly identical in measurement and the waist is about 10" smaller. Select styles that curve with the body. This figure can wear almost anything unless she is petite. Then scale is important.

Fashion and Fit

Once you determine shape and silhouette, you must establish your correct pattern size. Choosing the right size avoids the frustration of wasting time, money and effort. Often when fashion takes an abrupt turn, a new standard of fit emerges. This is the ideal time to re-establish your pattern size.

To be sure you are buying the correct pattern size, you should consider figure changes you may have experienced over the years. Though your actual weight may remain constant, subtle changes in body contours might require you to carefully re-evaluate the silhouettes and styles that are most becoming on you, and you might have to select a different size.

Follow these recommended steps for determining your correct pattern size: measure precisely, select your correct figure type, and understand the concept of design ease. With this knowledge, you can approach your next sewing project with confidence.

Accurate measurements are the starting point in selecting your correct pattern type and size. Four basic measurements are essential: chest/bust, waist, hip and back waist length. Additional measurements will be necessary if you have to make any pattern adjustments and alterations. The best pattern for you may also depend upon the garment type, your frame, personal taste and the degree of fashion fit.

What do you do if your measurements don't fall perfectly into one size? Choose the size by the garment type. For dresses, blouses, tops, jackets, coats and vests, select the size closest to your bust (or chest) measurement. Also, if there is more than 2" (5 cm) difference between your bust and chest measurements, select pattern size by your chest measurement because you will achieve a better fit through your shoulders, chest and upper back. Adjust the bust if necessary. (Patterns are designed to fit a B cup.) Adjust the pattern at waist and hips as needed.

For skirts, pants, shorts and culottes, select the size closest to your waist measurement if there is detailing in the waist area—such as pleats, tucks or darts—and adjust the hip. However, if your hips are proportionately larger than your waist—by 13" (33 cm) or more—select the size closest to your hip measurement. It's better to alter the waist than to try to add a dramatic amount to the hips.

If your measurements fall between two sizes, consider your bone structure. If you are thin and small-boned, choose the smaller of the two sizes. If you are larger-boned, choose the larger size. Personal preference may also influence your size selection, depending on whether you prefer a looser or closer fit.

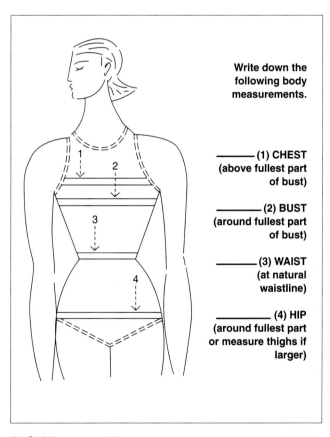

Write down the following body measurements.

———— (1) CHEST
(above fullest part of bust)

———— (2) BUST
(around fullest part of bust)

———— (3) WAIST
(at natural waistline)

———— (4) HIP
(around fullest part or measure thighs if larger)

Body Measurements
This drawing shows how and where to measure, and provides space for you to record your findings. When taking measurements, be sure you are wearing properly fitted undergarments and your usual shoes so that your posture will be normal. Make sure the tape measure is held straight and snug, but not tight, against the body.

Fashion and Fabric

When you are ready to put new pieces into your wardrobe, avoid the mistake of choosing an old style pattern and fabric that do not reflect today's fashion sense. You will look and feel outdated before you complete your sewing project. Look to the contemporary designers who have spent time and money testing fabrics and styles in their studios.

Plan your wardrobe additions carefully. New pieces should work with existing pieces; some should be neutrals and others accent colors. Build your base from the neutrals. Color accents give each outfit a "lift," and must work together.

For many sewers, fabric is a love affair of the senses—you fall in love with the print, the drape, the texture, the color, the feel or something it reminds you of. Before you get carried away, carefully assess how it will work for you. The fabric should add something to your wardrobe and extend your wardrobe dressing. It should be flattering to you in color, weight and texture. Consider also the versatility; buy 80% of your fabrics to wear nine months of the year. Lightweight wools, heavyweight cottons, rayons, silks and blends are ideal transitional fabrics that will take you more places, last for more months, and move from day to evening.

Sewing Essentials

A comfortable work space and the right equipment are absolutely essential for your sewing success. The suggestions here will get you off to a great start.

Your Work Space

Sewing can be the most disorganized and unmanageable project in your home if you haven't set up a special place for your sewing tools and equipment. Space in a closet, along a wall, or tucked in a corner of a room can become a convenient and comfortable sewing center if it is well-planned. Organized and accessible sewing equipment, projects and supplies are the key to more enjoyable and productive sewing.

A sewing center should include an area for stitching and pressing, and a table for project work. Working efficiency is important to the sewing space design, so it is ideal if you can arrange these elements in a triangle to minimize footwork. Place the pressing surface and project table on each side of the sewing machine in a U-shape arrangement. By pivoting in a chair with casters, you can remain seated and easily reach everything.

Storage of sewing equipment and supplies is important in creating a workable sewing center. You can use furniture designed as sewing cabinets, office and computer workstations; or modular units and cabinets for easy-access storage. Most of this furniture can integrate or camouflage your sewing center in another room in your home.

Plan your storage so it can be changed or expanded to meet your needs. Store items used most often with-in reach of the work area. Corkboards keep directions and small pattern pieces right at hand, and pegboards keep notions and small tools within easy reach.

Because sewing requires twice as much lighting as for reading, good lighting is essential. If possible, use a combination of natural and artificial light to prevent eyestrain. Eliminating shadows and high contrasts will reduce eye fatigue, so use both general room and task-specific lighting.

To work efficiently, design a convenient sewing space that includes areas where you can comfortably stitch, press, and have room for project work. For sewing equipment and supplies you need storage that is easily accessible and that can be changed or expanded. Sewing furniture is available in both contemporary and traditional designs.

The Right Equipment

Well-chosen tools and notions will make organized sewing easier and faster. Take time to discover the many different measuring, marking and pressing tools available to make your sewing more accurate.

CUTTING AND MARKING TOOLS

Invest in good quality shears, scissors, thread snips and rotary cutters; keep them clean and sharpened. Wrist pin cushions and magnetic pin holders keep sharp glass-head pins at your fingertips and off the floor. Sewing machine needles dull quickly; keep a good supply on hand.

A good assortment of tools includes seam gauges and stitching templates; pressure-sensitive, reinforced and extra-long tape measures; dressmaker's clear plastic rulers, yardsticks, T-squares and skirt markers; French, hip and flexible curves. Many varieties of marking tools help you transfer construction symbols from the pattern to the fabric. Make your marks with water-soluble and air-erasable vanishing pens, tailor's chalk or chalk wheels, wash-out pencils and wash-away thread, or tracing wheels and dressmaker's tracing paper. Always remember to test your fabric to see how removable the marker will be.

PRESSING TOOLS

Careful and thorough pressing can elevate your sewing project from the rank of amateur to professional. Invest in a quality iron that provides plenty of clean steam without leaking and dripping. For expert pressing, consider some of these key pressing tools: ham and ham holder, seam roll, press mitt and cloth, point presser and clapper, sleeve board, tailor board, and needleboard. As you follow the progression of sewing techniques described in the following chapters, note the important roles these pieces play.

MISCELLANEOUS SUPPLIES

Maintain a supply of commonly used notions: buttons, elastics, hooks and eyes, interfacings, linings, shoulder pads, threads and zippers.

SEWING EQUIPMENT

Read your sewing machine and serger manuals so you'll know each machine's capabilities. Follow the maintenance schedule to keep the machines in good working order. You will also find it useful to keep replacement parts on hand: bobbins, sewing machine bulbs and serger knives.

CHAPTER 2

Donna Karan

Donna Karan's design philosophy is founded on the principle of a "complete wardrobe" that takes a woman from season to season with a minimum of garments and a maximum of ensemble possibilities. Her clothes are modern, feminine and classic. They feel good to the wearer, flatter her figure, and reflect a marvelous combination of design, comfort and luxury.

Two of Donna Karan's trademark garments are a simple, unlined jacket and a bodysuit, both offering the wearer many wardrobe possibilities. In this chapter, you will learn great seam finishes for unlined jackets as well as the latest designer techniques for working with stretch fabrics to make your own bodysuit.

How to Build a Wardrobe

Building a basic wardrobe begins with a good jacket pattern. This seasonless, unlined jacket is versatile, and can be personalized with the use of a great fabric made to fit you and your attitude.

The Designer at Work

Donna Karan was literally born into the fashion world. Her father was a haberdasher, her mother a showroom model and fashion sales representative. While she was still in high school, Karan designed and made her first collection for a fashion show. While she was a student at Parson's School of Design, Anne Klein hired her as an assistant. She eventually became that company's chief designer, receiving the Coty Award three times and being honored with election to its Hall of Fame.

Ten years later, together with her husband, sculptor Stephen Weiss, Donna Karan launched her own company—DKNY—and debuted her first collection. The reaction from the press and retailers was enthusiastic enough to guarantee her a most promising future in international fashion.

Donna Karan is passionate about fabric. The fabrics in her clothing are made to her specifications and drapability is the key. Trademarks are luscious crepes, airy chiffons, supple knits and—frequently—fabrics with stretch. She says, "The fabrics I use must be terribly soft, cuddly enough for comfort and bold enough for swagger." Donna Karan cites the main key to her success is that she designs for herself—businesswoman, traveler, wife, mother, and recently, grand-mother. "I understand a woman's particular body problems, how to accent the best parts and de-emphasize the others. I know which items really work." And as her own life evolves, her other lines mirror her own wardrobe needs, beginning with the DKNY casual look, and branching out to lingerie, hosiery, fragrance, and men's and children's clothing.

Home sewers/designers with more ideas than time to execute them, take heart—Donna Karan has the same dilemma. "There's so much to be done. DKNY under-wear, swimwear, home furnish-ings…the designs are already in my head, it's just a matter of get-ting them executed." Donna Karan is delighted at the success of her designs with home sewing pat-terns. "It's marvelous that women will be sewing my clothes. They'll get the color, fit and attitude they want. It's a highly personalized approach to dressing. I find sewing to be a very creative art form. It's a compliment to me that they'll choose my designs."

Wardrobe Strategy

The key element in all Donna Karan designs is the fit and shap-ing for a feminine, flattering and comfortable look and feel. Seams and darts are curved to shape and define shoulder and waist, mini-mize hips.

The Donna Karan look is based most often on a jacket and her sig-nature bodysuit—a garment she has propelled into a modern wardrobe basic. A bodysuit elimi-nates the bulk and bother of tuck-ing in a top, and—combined with a matching skirt—can add the look of a dress. "Two pieces are easier to fit than one. Just add a belt for a more finished look," advises the designer.

Karan reveals her understanding of today's busy woman: she enjoys having a wardrobe that satisfies her creative and aesthetic needs, fits her life and budget, is uncompli-cated yet individual. Building a basic year-round wardrobe is made simple by combining pieces in sea-sonless fabrics and neutral colors.

Consider using one jacket pat-tern twice—one for cool weather, perhaps a wool crepe in a dark tone, and again for warm weather in raw silk or linen. One pair of Karan trousers in a color and fabri-cation that works with both jack-ets, and a skirt for each season, yield many wearing options. Combine with two bodysuits—one in silk crepe, one in fine wool jer-sey, and you have eight pieces that take you through a year of work and travel.

As for color, black and ivory are pure Karan classic. (When asked if she could choose but one fabric to work with she opted for black wool jersey.) Alternative neutrals are navy, taupe, browns, grays, or darks such as eggplant, steel blue and bark. One trick for selecting neutrals is to work with hair, eye color, skin tones and repeat your own natural coloring. Her favorite fabric options are wool crepe, trop-ical weight wool, muted tweeds, silk or linen. She advises to keep surface design and color subtle.

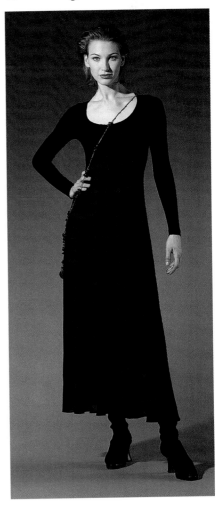

The Donna Karan look is often based on her signature bodysuit.

Seam Finishes for Unlined Jackets

An unlined jacket offers the benefits of less complicated construction than the lined jacket, as well as the extra mileage the wearer will get through several seasons of layering. However, for a quality unlined garment, you must finish the seams professionally. There are several great options you may choose.

PLAN THE CONSTRUCTION

Plan the construction and seam finish for an unlined jacket before cutting out the garment, and adjust your pattern accordingly. Thick, heavy fabrics may need slightly wider seam allowances to lie flat. Designers usually allow ³/₈"–1" (2 cm–2.5 cm) wide seams when using the Hong Kong finish, turned-and-stitched seams, Seams Great® or rayon seam binding. It is usually not necessary to add to the standard ⁵/₈" (15 mm) seam allowance when using a serged edge or an overlock foot.

On an unlined jacket, finished seams will usually be: shoulders, sides, sleeves, armholes, hems and facings. Test different finishes to determine the result you prefer.

Hong Kong Finish

Used in Hong Kong for fine custom-made clothing, this flat, narrow binding is a simple and elegant touch suitable for medium- to heavy-weight fabrics. The idea is to bind the seam in lightweight bias strips of fabric such as China silk, rayon lining, silk or polyester crepe de Chine. For the binding, cut 1¼" (3.2 cm) wide bias strips, piecing as necessary. (See Chapter 7 for tips on cutting and piecing bias strips.) Cut enough strips to bind both sides of all exposed seams. After cutting, press strips to remove stretch and prevent rippling. Bind after each seam is sewn, as you progress through the construction of the garment.

Hong Kong Finish, Step One
Attach binding to seam edge, with right sides together, ¹/₄" (6 mm) from edge, using a 2.5 stitch length (12 stitches per inch) and a size 12/80 needle. Press flat. Trim seam allowance to an even ¹/₈" (3 mm), using sharp shears or a rotary cutter. Press again, wrapping the binding around the raw seam edge to the wrong side.

Hong Kong Finish, Step Two
Working on the right side, stitch in the ditch of the seam, with the needle in the center position. On the wrong side, trim off excess binding ¹/₈" (3 mm) from stitching line. Because bias does not fray, the binding will not ravel.

Turned-and-stitched Finish

This traditional, clean, sturdy finish is suitable for light- to mid-weight flat fabrics which ravel: linen, poplin, denim, cotton or rayon gabardine. It works best on straight or only slightly curved seams. You may want to consider using a $3/4$"–$7/8$" (20 mm–22 mm) seam allowance for a $1/2$" (13 mm) finished seam. Test to be sure the impression of the seam will not show on the right side when pressed.

Seams Great® Finish

Seams Great is a product specially designed for home sewers, packaged in $5/8$" (15 mm) and $1 1/4$" (3.2 cm) widths in basic colors. This sheer knit binding curls in half when stretched, so it is easy to apply to the raw edge on a seam, hem or facing, and does not add bulk or change the drape of the fabric. Apply Seams Great before or after seams are sewn. Think about using a wider seam allowance—$3/4$"–1" (20 mm–25 mm), depending on your fabric. Seams Great works well for a range of fabrics from sheer silks to heavy woolens.

Seam Binding

Seam binding is a flat woven tape of rayon or polyester. When pressed in half to encase seams and hems, it is a thin and elegant finish for bulky and flat fabrics which fray—gabardine, linen, wool tweed. Seam binding gives a thinner, flatter edge than the Hong Kong finish; it requires only one line of stitching and two layers as opposed to two stitchings and three layers with the Hong Kong edge. However, it does not lend itself to curved edges. Purchase enough to bind both sides of seams. Press all the binding at once. With this technique, it is sometimes easier to finish seams before constructing the garment.

Zigzag Finish

Fine-tune the old-fashioned zigzag seam finish by using an overcast foot to prevent the fabric from "tunneling" or forming a ridge. Use a stitch length of 3 (10 stitches per inch) and width of 4. As a last resort, stitch *almost* but not quite at the edge of the fabric (this also prevents tunneling), and trim excess as needed. Finish the seam after it is sewn and pressed.

Turned-and-stitched Finish
Press the edge of the seam under $1/4$" (6 mm) to the wrong side; with right side up, top-stitch a scant $1/8$" (3 mm) from the edge. Press again.

Seams Great Finish
Pull Seams Great gently to determine the direction of curl, and wrap around raw edge of seam, keeping a slightly wider width on the underside of the seam. Pull while stitching close to the inside edge, catching the underside. Use either a straight stitch (2.5 length/12 stitches per inch) or zigzag stitch (2.5 length, 2.5 width).

Seam Binding Finish
Press binding in half lengthwise, with one side slightly wider than the other. Working with the right side of the fabric UP, place the narrow side of the binding on top when stitching. Stitch along the edge of the tape, using a 2.5–3 stitch length (10–12 stitches per inch), and applying a bit of tension so the tape wraps around and encases the raw edge.

Sewing Stretch Fabrics

When you think of the ideal contemporary wardrobe that feels great to wear, packs well, and will take you to office, evening, weekend and leisure pursuits, you probably include garments made of soft, stretchy knits. With the advent of the home serger and the availability of stretch fabrics in all weights and textures, you can create your own knit garments with a designer look.

Choosing the Fabric

Such recent innovations as Donna Karan's bodysuit have not only transformed modern dressing, but have introduced a new breed of knits and stretch fabrics. The key ingredient in nearly all these fabrics is Lycra® which offers supple drapability, stretch and excellent recovery. Making your own garments of Lycra blends is surprisingly simple and quick.

As a first step, be certain that your fabric has the right amount of stretch and recovery for the pattern. Use the Stretch Gauge on the back of the pattern envelope. The fabric should stretch easily and return to its original size without distortion. If your pattern calls for a two-way stretch knit, repeat this test on the lengthwise grain. Failure to follow these guidelines can result in a garment that is too small or will stretch out of shape.

Patterns designed for knits take the stretch into consideration; less ease is allowed. Do not use a woven fabric for a pattern labeled "for stretch knits only." If the pattern is labeled "for two-way stretch only," it usually requires a knit containing Lycra.

USING THE STRETCH GAUGE

Fold fabric on the crosswise grain at least 4" (10 cm) from the selvage. Holding the folded edge along the left end of the Stretch Gauge, gently stretch 4" (10 cm) of fabric as marked to the line on the far right. If your knit cannot easily stretch this distance, it may be unsuitable for the pattern.

NEEDLES AND THREAD FOR KNITS

Most medium-weight knits sew beautifully with good quality long-staple polyester thread and a new size 12/80 universal needle. If you encounter skipped stitches, change to a ballpoint needle which has a rounded tip that penetrates the fabric by piercing between—rather than through—the threads.

Although knits do not fray, knit seams must stretch without breaking the stitches. Knits and elastics may be sewn on a conventional sewing machine with merely a zigzag option, although stretch stitches and an overlock machine speed and simplify the process and give a beautiful professional finish. Play with your scraps to determine degree of stretch and best finish on both lengthwise and crosswise grain.

Sewing Machine

It's possible to sew stretch fabric successfully on a sewing machine that has zigzag capabilities. When you use a standard machine, remember not to stretch the fabric as you sew.

Stretch Seams on a Sewing Machine
Left to right: 1) Narrow zigzag (2.5 stitch length/12 stitches per inch and .5 stitch width). 2) Two rows of narrow zigzag; seam trimmed close to second row. 3) Two rows of zigzag, one narrow and one wide (3 stitch length/10 stitches per inch and 4 stitch width); trimmed seam. 4) and 5) Two examples of overcast options.

The Serger

The serger or overlock machine is the most exciting and important sewing tool since the invention of the sewing machine itself. A serged seam edge is one of the fastest, easiest and most professional ways to finish most seams. Test to see which width and thread combination works best with your fabric and to be sure that the impression of the thread does not show on the

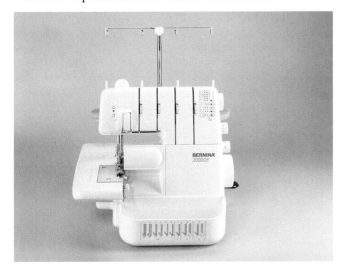

right side when the seam is pressed open. If this "strike-through" does occur, try a two-thread finish.

A three-thread edge with a 5 mm width and 2.5 length, using long-staple polyester or coned serger thread, is the most frequently used seam finish. Machine embroidery thread gives the lightest, finest finish—good for thin or flat fabrics. Texturized nylon thread or woolly nylon—soft and stretchy—is a good option for textured knits or stretchy wovens.

First, plan the order of construction. Using 5/8" (15 mm) seams, cut and fuse interfacing before serging. Serge only those seams which will be pressed open: on a jacket that would be the shoulder, side seams, sleeve cap and seams, armhole. Unless the fabric frays very easily, you should not serge enclosed seams: neck, collars, or front edge. Serge hems before or after the jacket is constructed.

STRETCH SEAMS

Use the serger to seam, finish, and trim all in one step. A balanced three-thread serged seam (length 2.5, width 5 to 7 mm) gives good stretch and recovery. Use long-staple polyester thread, overlock thread or woolly nylon in the loopers. Another option is the three-thread super stretch, a seam you can do on any three/four-thread serger. Use the two-thread converter and bypass the upper looper. The left needle thread forms loops on the underside, wrapping around the fabric edge—wonderful with woolly nylon. Use 2.5 stitch length, 2 cutting width, N-2 differential.

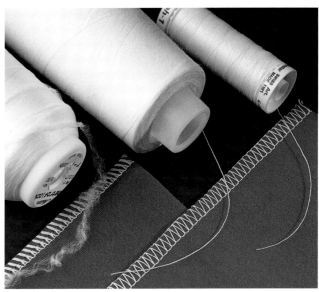

Stretch Seams on a Serger
Left: super-stretch seam with woolly nylon in loopers. Right: balanced three-thread seam.

Bodysuit Details

Once you've found the right bodysuit pattern for you, and a suitable stretch fabric, constructing the garment proceeds quickly and easily, even if you don't have a serger. Follow these tips for details that are unique to the bodysuit. Join the side seams of the bodysuit before sewing the leg openings, leaving crotch seam open.

Distributing Elastic on Leg Opening

Divide each leg opening in half; mark with pin or chalk. Divide elastic in half, marking in similar manner. Matching up these reference points, stitch elastic to garment, stretching to distribute most of fullness at the curved area in both front and back. Use a 1:1 ratio of fabric and elastic in the straight areas adjacent to crotch opening. Stretch elastic to fit the remaining curved areas, which should result in slightly more fullness at the leg back.

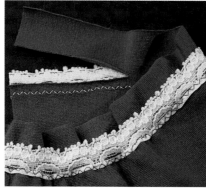

Exposed Elastic

Place the decorative edge of stretch lace along the seamline, wrong side of lace next to the right side of the fabric. Stitch close to the opposite edge, using a narrow zigzag (length 3, width 2). Trim the fabric close to the zigzag stitch, leaving the lace exposed as an attractive edge finish.

Exposed Elastic Edge, Part One

Position lingerie elastic or stretch lace with inner picot edge along seamline, wrong side of elastic/lace against right side of fabric. Using a narrow zigzag (length 3, width 2), stitch close to inner edge. Trim close to the stitching.

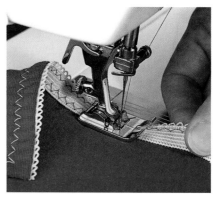

Exposed Elastic Edge, Part Two

Turn lingerie elastic to the inside, catching unsecured edge of elastic with a zigzag or multiple zigzag stitch. The scalloped or picot edge will be exposed.

ELASTICS

Consider these elastics for the leg opening on a bodysuit:

• 1/4" (6 mm) non-roll elastic that you stitch directly on the fabric.

• Clear "plastic" elastic, 1/4"–3/8" (6 mm–10 mm), designed for swimwear, but perfect for bodysuits, is soft, with 100% stretch recovery, and will not fray if serged or zigzagged to an edge.

• Lingerie elastic comes in 1/4" and 1/2" (6 mm and 13 mm) widths with a decorative picot edge, is supple and designed to be exposed.

• Donna Karan frequently uses stretch lace as a leg finish on her luxurious bodysuits. It's available in a variety of widths from 1/4"–7/8" (6 mm–22 mm).

Cut elastic 2"–3" (5 cm–7.5 cm) shorter than leg opening; stretch lace may require an even shorter length. All methods attach elastic to the leg opening, thus preventing rolling which may occur with a casing. Elastic may be encased or lie next to the body. It may be necessary to use a heavier ballpoint needle (size 14/90) when stitching through some elastic.

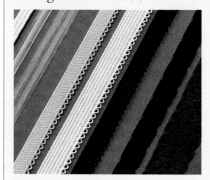

Elastics for Bodysuits

Left to Right: 1/4" (6 mm) non-roll elastic; clear elastic; lingerie elastic; stretch lace in 1/4" (6 mm) and 7/8" (22 mm) widths.

THE SERGER ELASTICATOR FOOT

This serger accessory foot stitches elastic to an edge, evenly stretching and gathering the elastic while trimming away excess fabric. A roller stretches the elastic during serging and holds it in place under the presser foot. The elasticator foot has a slot to insert $3/8"$–$1/2"$ (5 mm–12 mm) wide elastic or lace, and a screw adjustment to adjust for a tighter or looser gather. Run a test to determine the best tension and stitch length. Tighten screw at half and full revolutions when making your test. Precutting the elastic is not necessary when using the elasticator foot as long as you've made a satisfactory pre-test. Follow the guidelines for distributing fullness; as a general rule, use a looser tension on the front leg, tighter on the back leg. Duplicate tensions on both legs.

Finish on the sewing machine. Turn elastic to inside and stitch from the right side using a zigzag stitch or double-needle finish, making sure to catch the underside of the elastic.

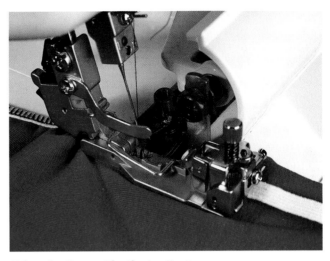

Using the Serger Elasticator Foot
Insert elastic into slot, then sew a few stitches to catch elastic, moving it to one side of the guide. Adjust screw to desired stretch. Place fabric under elasticator so that elastic is applied to the wrong side of the fabric. Elastic guides itself; you need to guide only the fabric. Use the right-hand needle position for narrow elastic, the left-hand needle position for wider elastic.

FINISHING THE BODYSUIT WITH SNAP TAPE

Snap tape with soft snaps is available by the yard in black and white—identical to what is used in ready-to-wear. Be sure to line up socket and ball strips so they will match when snapped. Apply tape after leg opening is finished. Donna Karan uses two rows of sockets on her ready-to-wear garments to allow for comfort.

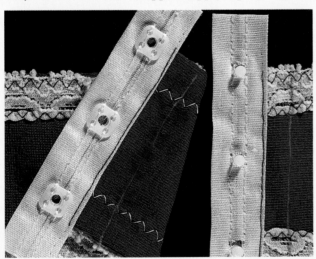

Snap Closure, Step One
Using a zipper foot, edgestitch wrong side of ball section of tape to right side of front crotch seam allowance, $1/4"$ (6 mm) from seamline as pictured. Stitch wrong side of corresponding socket section of tape to wrong side of back crotch seam allowance, $1/4"$ (6 mm) from the seamline.

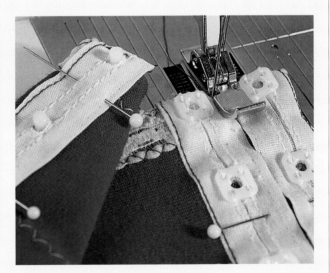

Snap Closure, Step Two
Turn both tapes, folding along tape edges, front ball section to inside, back socket section to outside, tucking under ends even with leg openings. (Center of each tape will be centered over seamline.) Edgestitch, using zipper foot. Stitch second socket section next to first section.

CHAPTER 3

Calvin Klein

C alvin Klein defines his fashion as "modern clothes for the modern woman." With clean lines and refined shapes, his designs are geared to the life style of the contemporary woman who demands versatile clothes for her varied schedule. While interpreting the mood of the times, Klein designs clothes that are adaptable, relaxed and casual, but never overpowering the woman who wears them.

Klein chooses luxurious materials—often silk, which has the hand and drape to show off his elegantly simple designs. In this chapter, you will learn how to handle the new "washed" silks, and get designer tips for another of Klein's signature looks—the denim blue jean—as well as techniques for fine, tailored details.

The Master of Modern Dressing

The supple shaping and soft silhouette of this loose-fitting, single-breasted jacket and slim pant in washed silk reflect Klein's relaxed approach to quality and cut. In this jacket, soft rounded shoulders, slim kimono sleeves and underarm gussets replace traditional set-in sleeves.

The Designer at Work

Klein, born and raised in New York, taught himself at an early age to sketch and sew. He claims to have made up his mind to be a clothing designer at age five! Throughout his education—at the High School of Art and Design, and the Fashion Institute of Technology—he focused his ambition on designing and owning his own business.

The story of his first big sale is fascinating: soon after he and friend Barry Schwartz began their coat company in 1968, a buyer from Bonwit Teller stepped off the elevator at the wrong floor of the York Hotel and chanced upon Klein's workroom. Impressed by what he saw, he placed an order for $50,000. Building upon this serendipitous success, the world of Calvin Klein now includes several divisions each for women's and men's wear, his famous jeans, intimate apparel, footwear, accessories, hosiery, swimwear and fragrances. Klein was the youngest person ever to receive the Coty Award, a distinction he enjoyed for three consecutive years.

Klein interprets the moods of a new generation while anticipating a new century. He adapts his vision to meet a new attitude in fashion— off-beat, original, irreverent, relaxed, independent and willful. Today he stands at the pinnacle of international success. Says Klein,

"It's so much fun to love what you're doing. I'm a crazy perfectionist. It's really hard to please me. But when I do achieve it, I'm flying."

Klein's Favored Fabrics

Klein offers a distinctively American sense of style. "Everything begins with the cut," Klein says, pointing out that line and shape determine the function and beauty of any design. Klein also insists on the finest quality in fabrics of natural fibers: silk, cotton, wool, mohair and cashmere, as well as leather and suede. The rich texture of fine materials, combined with a palette of muted colors, completes the signature of Klein's silhouettes, at once practical and luxurious.

Klein's designs have been described as minimalist. Uncluttered styles call for fabrics to be the stars of the show. No other fabric has exactly the elegant drape or the subtle luster of silk. Long considered the ultimate luxury fabric, silk once was reserved for very dressy or formal wear, and had the reputation of fragility. New innovations in the finishing process of silk now make it a practical fabric for career dressing and sportswear. Klein has been a pioneer in this trend.

Denim is the quintessential American fabric, invented for working people. In one of the greatest ironies in fashion history, denim made a 180° turn in the late 20th century and became a status symbol, personified in the designer jean. Once again, Klein was the first designer to put his name and personal style to the jean. The look of denim is as durable as the fabric itself, and shows no letdown in popularity. Not content to relegate denim to pants only, designers have used denim for everything from glamorous, bejewelled evening jackets to interior decor.

These simple and clean silhouettes in refined earth tones exemplify Klein's ability to design separates that are stylish, functional and enduring. The straight-legged pants feature double-welt pockets, a designer detail you will learn in this chapter.

Sewing with Washed Silks

Washed silk and other fluid fabrics require new construction techniques and inner shaping components. Follow these suggestions and you'll be able to indulge yourself in these gorgeous fabrics now available for home sewing.

Silk's Characteristics

Washed silk comes in a wide variety of fabrications; the most popular versions available are China silk, habutai, douppioni, charmeuse and broadcloth. Washed silk yardage has been pre-treated in either a chemical bath or with fabric softeners to "alter" the fiber and create a sueded hand. Washing does not change the nature or care requirements of the silk fiber, but does change the hand and look of the cloth.

Silk is synonymous with luxury, and appreciated for its fluid drape and eager receptivity to brilliant dyes.

Pre-washing a sample swatch of your purchased silk yardage provides you an opportunity for controlling changes in the color, texture, size, sheen and hand.

Silk accepts dye well, but cannot be made color-fast without harming the fibers. Most silks lose some color in sunlight and laundering. The greatest color change occurs in the more intense and brighter colors. In addition, most silks get softer after washing and drying. Some lose their surface sheen after careful hand washing; most lose their sheen and acquire the sueded look after going through the tumbling action of a dryer.

Every type of silk shrinks somewhat. Testing and pre-shrinking ensures that you have enough fabric to complete a particular project. If your garment is going to be maintained by hand washing, all its components must be washable as well, and should be preshrunk. Garments with complex construction or details such as the Calvin Klein jacket and pants on page 30, are best dry cleaned, even when they are made of washable silk. Always pre-shrink fabric for a garment that will be dry cleaned. Thoroughly steam fabric on the wrong side, setting the iron on "low wool" and using a press cloth to protect the finish and avoid water spotting. Check straightness of the grain and avoid stretching silk while pressing.

Interfacings for Silk

Quality silks demand quality interfacings. Batiste, organza and sew-in tricot are ideal choices; they are lightweight, adding support but not stiffness. Most fusible interfacings are not recommended on silks because the resins will "bleed" through the silk during fusing and because the two fabrics acting as one will inhibit silk's natural drape. However, if the desired effect is to give more body to facings, test a silk scrap with a very fine fusible batiste or "cool-fuse" interfacing specifically designed to bond at a low temperature and maintain some drape.

Cutting Silk

Before you cut out your silk garment, prepare the cutting surface by taping tissue paper, examining paper or alpha-numeric pattern paper to your table. Fold fabric with the right sides together. Always use "with nap" layouts. Do not allow your fabric to hang off your table while cutting, as this could pull the fabric off grain. Cut through fabric in long, even strokes with micro-serrated dressmaker's shears or in a smooth, continuous line with a rotary cutter.

Marking Silk

You may choose one of several options to safely mark construction symbols. 1) Snip notches and folds in the seam allowance. 2) Pin-mark dots and darts using pins with small heads. Place pins through pattern tissue and both layers of fabric at interior symbols. Turn piece over and insert additional pins at each pin. Carefully remove pattern tissue, then separate the two layers and secure the pin points back into the fabric. 3) If garment will not be constructed immediately, mark with tailor's chalk on the wrong side of the fabric at each pin, then remove the pins. Be sure to test markings on a scrap of fabric to see that markings show, then disappear as expected. 4) If the chalk does not disappear satisfactorily, tailor's tacks with silk thread are an option. 5) A smooth-edge tracing wheel without tracing paper will leave a crease mark. Place pattern and fabric on a hard surface, cover area to be marked with a clear plastic storage bag, then apply firm pressure over area to be marked.

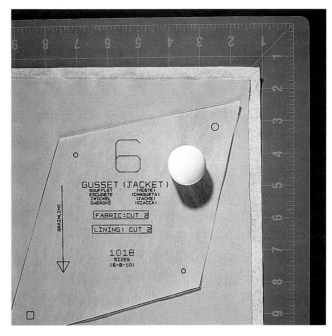

Cutting Out Silk on Paper
To eliminate slippage while cutting, weight silk fabric to paper, taking care to keep selvages and grain straight.

Sewing With Silk

You can eliminate most common problems with sewing silk by using the right notions and machine settings. Begin each project with a new machine needle: try size 9/65 or 10/70 for lightweight silks and size 12/80 for medium weights. Although good quality, sharp dressmaker silk pins will not leave holes or snag the yarns, it is still a good idea to pin pieces within the seam allowance. Never sew over the pins. Cotton-wrapped polyester thread and 100% silk-finish cotton (such as Mettler®) are best suited to sewing silk because they are weaker than the silk fibers and will break at stress points rather than "cut" the fabric yarns.

Use a machine stitch length of 3 (10 stitches per inch). To avoid puckering and to allow seams to be more supple, maintain a loose and well-balanced machine tension.

Sewing with Denim

Denim has been a popular fabric throughout the 20th century, embodied in the blue jean. Now designer labels have increased the price of blue jeans tenfold, and we see denim used in evening wear, sportswear, upholstery and wall coverings. Denim has proven to be one of the most durable fashion fabrics.

Flattering Jeans

Pants can camouflage or exaggerate figure problems, so it is important to choose a flattering style and establish a comfortable fit. Since straight-legged jeans will skim over most bumps and bulges, they have become a perennial favorite. If you already own a pair of jeans

The popularity of Calvin Klein signature jeans has struck a cord with women of all ages. There are no gimmicks, no overt fashion trends, but an attitude and status symbol to be worn from a Friday evening social event to Saturday chores. Klein's jeans do not automatically become dated with each new fashion season. Whether the jeans are slim or full, they flatter in a subtle, sophisticated manner with their classic design and figure-enhancing fit.

that fit you well, you can use these to help you adjust your pants pattern. In any case, you will need to know your measurements to establish your size and determine which adjustments to make.

Accurate fitting can be time-consuming and requires precise measuring, flat pattern adjusting and detailed fitting but is rewarding because you need do this major work only once. Wear proper undergarments and shoes when taking measurements. Be accurate and honest, recording all data on a chart.

Refer to a fitting text to learn which measurements are important and how to take them precisely. Determine your size by your waist measurement unless your hips are much larger or smaller than that shown with the waist size. Compare your measurements with the actual pattern dimensions—taking ease into account—to determine if you'll have to make any adjustments in the pattern. (Many patterns are now marked in the hip area with the total garment measurement to make this process easier.) If you need to make major adjustments to customize your pattern, again refer to a fitting text to guide you through the steps.

Denim's Characteristics

Denim comes in a number of weights with a variety of finishes. Originally denim was 100% cotton, but now polyester and Lycra® blends are available. Distressed denims are created by stone- or sand-washing. These processes break down the surface fibers to make a lighter, softer hand and color. Napped denim is created by brushing the fabric surface to give a flannel-like feeling. New variations appear every season.

Always pre-treat denim before cutting. Most denims will shrink considerably, especially in the lengthwise direction of the grain. Repeated washings will remove excess dye and soften the fabric.

Sewing Techniques for Denim

Always cut your pattern using a "with nap" layout. Make test seams with your fabric scraps. If your stitches cause the seam to pucker, shorten the stitch length. If the fabric waves out of shape along the seam, lengthen the stitches. Stitch with the grain to prevent stretched seams.

JEANS NEEDLE AND FOOT

Use a size 14/90 jeans needle for medium-weight denim, and a 16/100 or 18/110 for heavy-weight denim. The jeans needle has a sharp point that penetrates closely-woven fabrics without breaking, and a large enough eye to accommodate heavy topstitching thread.

Use a jeans foot for sewing straight-stitch seams and stitching over thick seams. This foot has a flat underside with a short straight groove to ensure straight stitching. The needle hole is round to offer needle support, and the toes of the foot are notched for topstitching reference.

FELLING FOOT

Flat-felled seams provide a neat finish and help simulate the look of ready-to-wear. Make a flat-felled seam in medium-weight denims using a felling foot. This foot has a needle hole to support the needle, a straight groove the length of the foot on the underside to allow for bulk, and a bend to keep the fabric turned under when topstitching.

For the first step, pin two fabric edges with wrong sides together, with the lower piece extending approximately 3/8" (10 mm) beyond the upper one (read your machine manual to check the exact amount specified for your machine's particular foot). Fold this extension over the upper piece, then slide fabrics under the presser foot. Move needle position half left, and sew a few stitches. Leave the needle in the fabric, raise the foot, guide the fabric into the foot, and continue sewing the seam. (You should be sewing through three layers of fabric.) Open out fabric and press the seam flat so the fold covers the raw edge. Stitch down the folded edge.

Jeans Needle and Foot
When using a jeans needle, adjust stitch length to 2.5–3 (10–12 stitches per inch). Use a jeans foot to guard against bent and broken needles while sewing seams and topstitching. Use an edgestitching foot when stitching close to a fold or edge.

Felling Foot
For the second row of stitches, guide the fold into the foot again and sew another row of stitching parallel to the first row. Pull the fabric slightly on either side while sewing.

Sewing Tools for Denim

One of the common frustrations of working with denim is the difficulty of sewing over multiple thicknesses of fabric, such as the point where a flat-felled seam is hemmed. Because denim garments usually feature contrasting topstitching, it's a challenge to execute perfectly parallel lines of stitching. Fortunately, there are devices to assist you with these problems.

THE HUMP JUMPER

The hump jumper eliminates skipped stitches, stitches of uneven length and broken needles. This little device keeps the presser foot horizontal, thus allowing the fabric to maintain contact with the feed dogs for consistent stitching. It does not attach to the machine, so it is adaptable to various makes and models.

TOPSTITCHING GUIDES

Three types of topstitching guides can help you sew perfect, straight, professional-looking topstitching. A small magnetic guide is designed to be placed on the throat plate of a sewing machine at any width for consistent, straight stitching.

Most sewing machines have a curved guide that fits into a standard screw hole for attachments on the bed of the machine. Adjust and pivot it to accommodate the curve you will sew.

Guides for sewing the perfect fly front topstitching are available in see-through plastic. Position one of the four different widths over the zipper with the guide teeth placed along the center front seam. You can indicate the stitching line with a chalk marker or disappearing pen, then stitch, or you can use a zipper foot and sew next to the guide through all layers. For jeans, topstitch again 1/4" (6 mm) from first stitching.

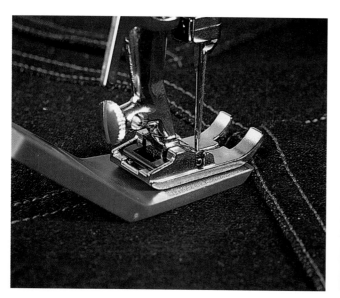

Hump Jumper
To ease the presser foot over a particularly thick spot, slip a hump jumper between the back of the presser foot and the fabric.

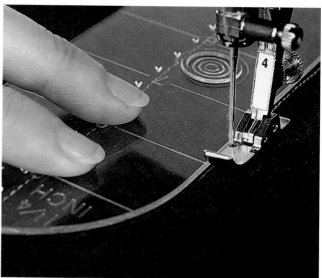

Fly Topstitching Guide
Topstitching with a zipper foot is foolproof when you use the edge of a plastic fly front template as a guide. Four widths are available in two plastic guides.

Tailored Details

Here are two fabulous tailored and practical details—the underarm gusset and the double welt pocket—that give otherwise simple garments that extra couturier touch.

Gussets

When a garment with a kimono sleeve is designed to fit close to the body, a gusset is necessary to reduce the strain under the arm and provide ease of movement. A gusset is a small piece of fabric inserted in the underarm of a garment to provide strength and comfort. It is set into a slash or seam that cuts across the garment from front to back under the arm. Many sewers are confused and apprehensive about gussets. However, if you accurately follow these logical steps to ensure appropriate reinforcement and stitch carefully, you are practically guaranteed foolproof results.

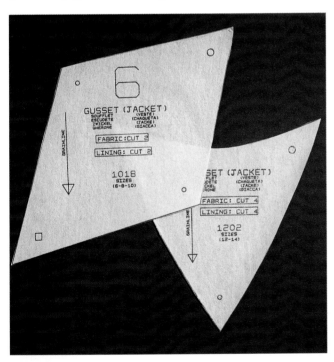

Gusset Styles
Gussets may be cut in one piece—diamond-shaped (left) , on the bias to ease underarm strain and allow a natural drape and stretch. Another style of gusset is the two-piece triangular gusset (right), with a seam joining the two sections, forming a diamond shape like the singular gusset.

REINFORCING THE GUSSET

Reinforce the garment before you slash it. Cut four 2" (5 cm) bias squares of lining remnant or self fabric (if it is firm and lightweight). Mark slash points and stitching lines on your garment in a method appropriate to your fabric.

Center the bias squares over slash points and stitching lines on the right side of the front and back pieces. Pin or baste in place, depending upon the slipperiness of your fabric. Stitch along stitching lines, using a short stitch length of .5–1.5 (15–20 stitches per inch), to the slash point, pivot and take one stitch, then pivot again and stitch along the remaining side.

Cut between stitching lines right up to each point. Press each side of the reinforcement towards the slashed edge. Turn reinforcements to the wrong side of garment so they can be treated as a seam allowance while you are stitching the gusset in place.

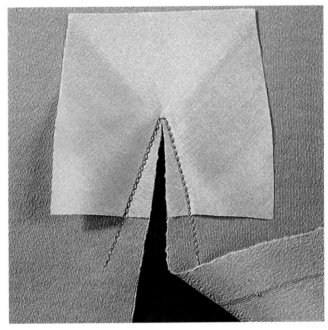

Gusset Reinforcements
Take care to stitch close to the slash point, pivoting twice, and allowing the space of one short stitch across the slash point.

ATTACHING THE GUSSET

Before attaching the gusset, stitch garment side seams and sleeve seams, ending stitching at markings indicated on your pattern. Press seams open. The unstitched area under the arm accommodates the gusset. Pin or baste gusset to right side of front, back and sleeves, matching seamlines. From the garment side, sew gusset to garment, pivoting carefully at the point as you did for the gusset reinforcement, treating the reinforcement patch as seam allowance. End stitching at seams or

Attaching the Gusset
Take small stitches as you stitch alongside the previous stitching at the reinforcements. Begin at the seams or markings and pivot at the slash points.

Finishing the Gusset
Press seams of gusset so they lie flat, giving a neat appearance and smooth feeling under the arm. Edgestitch.

markings, being sure not to catch the side seam allowances of the garment in the stitching.

FINISHING THE GUSSET

Pull all thread ends to wrong side of gusset and knot together. Trim reinforcements to ³/₈" (10 mm). To further strengthen the gusset on sporty or casual clothes, edgestitch the gusset seam on the right side of fabric. If garment is to be lined, no further finishing or trimming of the edges is necessary.

Welt Pockets

A slashed pocket with a double welt looks like a large bound buttonhole and is constructed in a similar manner. Two narrow welts are applied to a slashed area of the garment, with a pocket attached to the inside edge of the welts.

Double-welt pockets that appear in today's ready-to-wear clothing have a lightweight fusible interfacing stabilizing the pocket area of the garment. The interfacing, cut out with pinking shears, is approximately one inch larger all around than the finished welt pocket. Test your interfacing to see if it works on your chosen fabric.

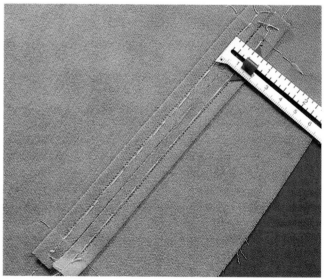

Welt Placement
Position the cut edges of the welts on the right side of the fabric along the center placement line; pin. Folded edges should be 1" (25 mm) apart; basting stitches should be ¹/₂" (13 mm) apart. Mark ends of pocket on welts. Hand-baste to control stretching and slipping. Using a short stitch length of 1 (18 stitches per inch), machine-stitch the welts along the basting lines. Begin and end your stitching exactly at the corner markings; backstitch.

ATTACHING THE WELTS

Turn garment to the right side and precisely mark the center slash (welt placement line) and ends (corners) of pocket on the right side of fabric, using a chalk wheel, wax or thread bastings, and a see-through ruler. This is essential to make your construction procedure easier.

Cut the welt pieces 1" (25 mm) longer than the pocket opening, and 1 1/8" (2.5 cm) wide. Cut, steam and stretch the welts to eliminate shrinking and puckering later. Fold the welts in half lengthwise, with wrong sides together; press. Machine-baste 1/4" (6 mm) from the welt fold and trim raw edges so folded welts are exactly 1/2" (13 mm) wide.

Slashing the Welt

Working from the wrong side of the garment, slash carefully along the slash line between the two rows of stitching. Stop 1/2" (13 mm) from each end, then clip diagonally to the last stitch of each welt. Press flat, then turn welts through the opening to the inside. Check to see that welts are straight and even. Steam and finger-press, eliminating puckers. Tuck the remaining short raw edges of welt opening inside. With silk thread, whipstitch welts together; press.

PREPARING POCKET PIECES

For horizontal double-welt pockets, cut rectangular pocket pieces from lining or pocketing scraps. Cut piece "A" 6 1/2" (16.5 cm) wide and 7 1/2" (19 cm) long; this piece attaches to and hangs from the lower welt. Cut piece "B" 6 1/2" (16.5 cm) wide and 8" (20.5 cm) long; this piece attaches to the upper welt and hangs behind both welts. Prepare a self-fabric underlay or facing and attach it to the top of piece B.

For *vertical* double-welts use curved pattern pieces adapted from an inseam pocket pattern. Cut one pocket

piece from lining fabric and one from garment fabric, the latter with a 1/2" (13 mm) straight side extension deep enough to lay under the welts. For pants or skirts make an upper extension high enough to reach into the waist seam.

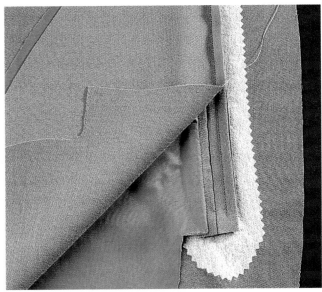

Attaching Pocket Lining

Pin the top edge of pocket piece A over the bottom welt, matching cut edges. With lining side down, stitch over previous stitching line. Keeping pocket piece A free, pin the top edge of pocket piece B to the edge of the top welt. Again with lining side down, stitch over previous stitching line. Press each piece towards the front.

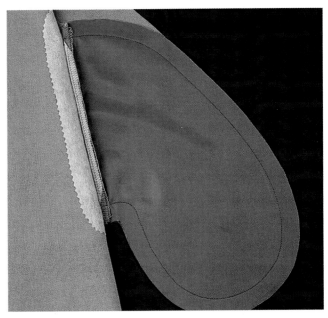

Finishing Welt

Place garment wrong side up on a flat surface; flatten pocket. Fold garment back to adjust pocket edges and expose welts. Pin around pocket from the upper to the lower part of welt. From the lining side, stitch pocket pieces together, catching ends of welts and triangular ends of welt opening; backstitch over them securely.

CHAPTER 4

Linda Allard for Ellen Tracy

From its modest beginning as a blouse company founded by Herbert Gallen in 1949, the Ellen Tracy Company has blossomed into a successful organization by paying attention to the needs of women. As a working woman designing for women, Linda Allard, Director of Design, embodies the Ellen Tracy customer. She understands today's clothing needs for a busy life style.

Linda Allard considers the jacket an essential wardrobe component. In this chapter you'll find out how Allard creates three different ensembles, using one jacket as a pivotal garment. You'll learn designer techniques for sewing knits and altering waistlines.

Ellen Tracy's Wardrobing Concept

The long, unlined duster coat is a jacket taken to a new length but can be worn as a dress. The jacket is the key element in Ellen Tracy's concept of wardrobing—four pieces become three ensembles for work or play.

The Designer at Work

Right after her graduation in 1962 as a Fine Arts major, Linda Allard was hired by Herbert Gallen at Ellen Tracy to be his design assistant. Two years later, she was named Director of Design, and with Gallen, began developing concepts for the evolution of the Ellen Tracy Company.

By 1975, when the junior market entered the work force in large numbers, clothing needs changed, so the company decided to move its focus into contemporary departments and finally into the "bridge" market—which caters to the upscale career woman—where it has become a mainstay. This sharp business decision allowed the company's sales volume to triple in the last decade. Linda Allard's name was added to the Ellen Tracy label in 1984. Under Allard's artistic leadership, Ellen Tracy is synonymous with exclusive, high-quality fabrics, unique color stories, and the concept of the total wardrobe for the working woman.

Ellen Tracy has continued to identify shifting demographics and standards through the years. A petites division was introduced in 1983, then a very successful dress division in 1985. A new label—"Company," targeting a more leisure-oriented customer—was introduced in 1991. And in 1993, the large sizes division was launched and the dress division was expanded to include evening wear. Scarves, belts, shoes, eye wear, hosiery, handbags, and fragrance are some of the accessories under licensing agreements.

The Total Look

Linda Allard and Ellen Tracy represent the philosophy of the "total look." When designing a season's line, Allard starts with great pieces and puts them together like a puzzle.

You can plan your wardrobe like that, too. Starting with a jacket, choose pants that have the right leg width to go with the cut and length of the jacket. Change the mood with a flippy skirt or a tailored skirt, play with the idea of the new drapy shorts, or wear the jacket with a dress. Many patterns offer many views within one pattern envelope, and you, too, can develop many ensembles by using multiple Ellen Tracy patterns.

The Ellen Tracy wardrobe is a beautiful balance between tailored and feminine. Menswear fabrics such as wool gabardine, pinstripes and tweed suitings are mixed with silk suede, crepe de Chine and georgettes. Color combinations are unusual; for example, oregano with plum. Allard keeps swatches on hand and, at the beginning of each season, plays with new combinations of textures, colors and fabrics. Classic garments can be personal-

ized by the addition of the right shoes, scarves and belts.

Allard says there are a few key pieces in any wardrobe—a black turtleneck sweater, a white shirt, a pair of trousers, and two good jackets, one in black or your favorite neutral and the other in your best color. From this core, you start the building process, adding pieces each season and changing color combinations from time to time.

The Jacket

Ellen Tracy is well-known for jackets. The jacket is a pivotal wardrobe piece and one that is essential for business women. As an important "power piece," it must have longevity and may be the costliest fashion investment in a wardrobe.

Ellen Tracy jackets make a woman feel good about how she looks. Linda Allard is known for her innovative color combinations and quality fabrics, details and workmanship. Her jackets are fresh each season with a variety of looks. A long, unlined duster coat is a jacket taken to a new length. A shirt made in drapy, fluid fabrics becomes a jacket when belted. Allard's well-known, traditional tailored jackets are more constructed and move closer to the body in leaner silhouettes. The boxy, relaxed easy jacket has a minimum of darts and seams.

The same duster coat becomes a long tunic when worn open as a jacket over pants, with the addition of a wide-collared blouse.

The duster coat is now an integral part of a third ensemble when added to a skirt of similar length and the same wide-collared blouse.

JACKET ESSENTIALS

To choose a jacket for you requires that you carefully study your body type and consider the needs of your lifestyle.

No matter what the silhouette, a good jacket starts with the shape and fit of the shoulders. What happens below is a matter of personal choice and types of inner construction—from the slouchy, softer approach to the constructed, menswear feel.

Ellen Tracy has a few suggestions for choosing a quality jacket. Designers begin with the shoulder pad. Since exaggerated shoulders are passé, today's shoulder pads are meant to be extensions of your natural shoulder line. Pads are essential, even in the new slouchy silhouettes, and often are designed to slope off the shoulder to accentuate the slouch. The jacket should sit squarely with the seams running down the center of your shoulders.

The collar should lie smoothly around your neck.

The number of stitches per inch indicates quality. Check this by bending your arm forward; if you can see stitches, it is inferior in quality. The sleeve setting should be free of puckers.

Ease of movement is important. The armholes are set higher in the newer styles to allow you to reach up without taking the whole jacket with you. And do not forget to cross your arms with your elbows together to make sure you have enough ease across the back for comfortable, all-day wearing.

And finally, use a good dry cleaner. Nothing can ruin the look of a jacket more than too much pressing or the wrong treatment.

CHOOSING A JACKET STYLE FOR YOU

Because the jacket is the key component in a wardrobe, it is important to choose a silhouette that is flattering to your figure. Fashion trends in jackets come and go, but it is better to stay with what works best for you from season to season and ease into fashion changes by modifying the look.

In Chapter 1, four basic figure shapes are described—inverted triangle, triangle, rectangle, and hourglass. First determine your basic silhouette, then choose the appropriate jacket style.

The **Inverted Triangle** figure type needs to minimize the bust and midriff area by choosing a jacket with a raglan sleeve to

draw the eye down. Another good choice is a soft wrap jacket with a belt to widen the hip. Avoid short lengths, large sleeves, and top details such as wide lapels, epaulets, and upper patch pockets. Fabrics should be soft and drapy.

The **Triangle** shape should strive to lessen the hip and thigh area and add fullness above the waistline, avoiding the raglan sleeve line. Instead, a straight jacket with a shoulder pad is more flattering, especially in a length that is either shorter or longer than the widest part of the hip. Upper details such as embellished lapels, soft folds at the shoulder line, and extended shoulders work well.

The **Rectangle** figure looks best

in a sculptured jacket that either introduces subtle shaping or bypasses the waistline altogether. Try a semi-fitted jacket with a shawl collar or a collarless cardigan with a continuous vertical seam in the front band, in longer lengths. Avoid wide, square shapes, boxy patch pockets, and horizontal seams and details including belts.

The **Hourglass** figure needs to be elongated and the curves softened by using soft, fluid fabrics. A jacket with a flared peplum and soft fullness or an asymmetrical closure emphasizes the waist. Avoid boxy jackets, patch pockets, and special design motifs at the bust and hip.

SHOULDER STYLES

The successful fit of any jacket, dress or top begins at the shoulder line, which must support the weight of the garment. The description on the back of the pattern envelope includes information about shoulder styles. This information helps you select the appropriate design for your figure type as well as the style and size of the shoulder pad to use, and allows you to determine your personal preference.

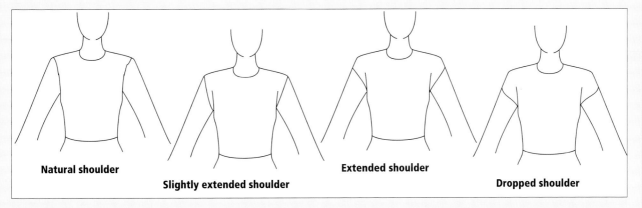

Natural shoulder

Slightly extended shoulder

Extended shoulder

Dropped shoulder

For a proper fit, shoulder seams of a jacket should not pull to either the front or the back. The fabric must lie smoothly without pulls or wrinkles. You may need to adjust your pattern for the slope and roll of your shoulders, working from the top down.

Knowing what kind of shoulder style the pattern designer had in mind helps you judge the appropriate selection for you. The above illustrations show the shoulder styling variations as noted on the pattern envelopes.

The **Natural Shoulder** line extends from the neck base to the arm hinge—i.e. the bone at the end point of your natural shoulder line. Because this is considered standard shoulder styling, it won't be mentioned in the pattern description.

The **Slightly Extended Shoulder** line extends beyond the natural shoulder by ¼"–¾" (6 mm–20 mm). Its crisp, angular shaping is usually enhanced by shoulder pads.

The **Extended Shoulder** line extends ⅞"–1½" (22 mm–3.8 cm) beyond the natural shoulder line. It, too, has crisp, angular shaping often enhanced by shoulder pads.

The **Dropped Shoulder** line has a rounded shape and falls 1⅝" (4 cm) or more beyond the normal shoulder. If your pattern was designed for shoulder pads, it will be noted, and the pad size listed on the pattern envelope. Extra room has been built into the pattern to accommodate the pad.

Do not attempt to change the shoulder styling with pattern adjustments; you may set off a chain of errors. The sleeve cap will not ease correctly, the armhole will be the wrong shape, sleeve length will be affected, and the entire garment will drape off-grain. You might spoil the balance, harmony, and proportions of the original design.

Fashion trends will determine whether a large, heavily padded shoulder or a softer, more natural look will be emphasized. The natural and slightly extended shoulders are considered more traditional for fitted and semifitted jackets, and often appear somewhat formal. The extended and dropped shoulders are more casual and comfortable, and work well with fluid fabrics and knits.

Waistline Treatments

H ow waistlines are constructed strongly affects both the style and comfort of a skirt or trousers. You probably already know your preferences; here are ways of changing existing patterns to suit them.

Skirts and Pants

MEASURING YOUR WAISTLINE

First, define your waistline with a piece of elastic. Keeping one finger behind the tape, measure your waistline and add 1" (25 mm) for ease.

ADJUSTING PATTERN FOR ELASTIC WAIST

Pants or skirts with front darts and a rigid waistband may not be flattering on all figures, nor are they as comfortable to wear as an elastic-waist pant or skirt. You can convert any pant or skirt pattern to a pattern with an elastic waist.

Tape the front and back tissue pattern pieces to larger pieces of pattern tracing cloth or plain paper. On the tissue pattern pieces, ignore the front and back darts and the zipper opening. From the widest part of the hip, draw a straight line up to the waistline with a pencil or marker. The waist opening should measure slightly larger than your hip measurement. Above the waistline add an amount twice the

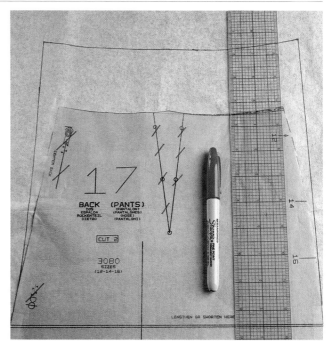

Adjusting the Pattern

Using a transparent ruler, draw new side seams parallel to the grainline (at a right angle to the horizontal adustment lines, as shown). Add the desired casing amount at the top edge of the pattern.

width of the elastic, plus ¾" (20 mm). This makes a "cut-on" waistband, not a separate one, and allows sufficient fabric for ease in the casing width and for finishing the inside raw edge. For example, for a finished 1" (25 mm) elastic band, extend the line up from the waist stitching line 2¾" (7 cm). Make sure the top edges of the front and back connect with one another in a smooth line.

When constructing pants, sew seams in this order: side seams, inner leg seams and crotch seam.

Edge-finish the top raw edge of waist by serging with a three-thread stitch formation. The serging finishes the edge nicely, allows for some "give" in a knit, and prevents the edges of woven fabric from raveling. Complete the casing and insert the elastic.

ADDING A WAISTBAND

Some patterns have waistline facings instead of a waistband, but you may wish to add a band for comfort and the option of wearing a belt, or perhaps the style is more flattering for your figure. To do this, eliminate the facing and create a band piece.

Measure your waist and add 1" (25 mm) for ease. Cut a rectangle of fabric to equal your waist measurement plus 1" (25 mm) for ease and 3½" (9 cm) for underlap and seam allowances. To determine width, use a pre-cut fusible waistband interfacing such as Perfo-fuse® that has one-half of the strip wider than the other half and is perforated at the foldline; measure the total width of the interfacing, and add ⅝" (15 mm) seam allowance. Fuse the widest side of the interfacing to one edge of your fashion fabric, leaving a ⅝" (15 mm) seam allowance on the other edge. Edge-finish the widest side of the band by serging or using seam binding.

The top of the unfinished pant or skirt should be 1" (25 mm) larger than the finished waistline measurement of the garment. This allows for the curve of the body just below the waistline. Mark center front and side seams on your waistband, dividing the extra 1" (25 mm) for ease into ¼" (6 mm) for each quarter of the waistband.

With right sides together, sew the waistband to the top of the garment along the edge of the interfacing, easing garment fullness. Trim and grade seams, leaving garment seam allowance widest. Press seam toward waistband. Fold waistband to the inside and edgestitch or stitch-in-the-ditch to catch the long edge of the band on the backside. Attach hook and eye fasteners.

CONVERTING TO A FACING

Sometimes you may want to eliminate the waistband and finish with a facing. This is one of Ellen Tracy's signature details.

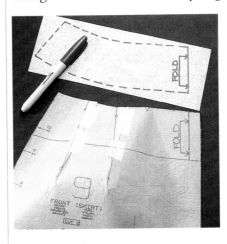

Drawing Facing Patterns
On the front and back pattern pieces, fold out the darts and tape down. Draw a line from center front to side seam and center back to side seam approximately 2⅝" (6.7 cm) down from the top edge of the pattern piece. Using a piece of plain tissue paper, trace the front and back facing pattern pieces, marking the straight of grain and foldline at center front. Using these new pieces as your facing, cut out your fashion fabric and interfacing.

Attaching Facings
Stay the facing waist seamline with ribbon seam binding or twill tape, placing one edge ⅛" (3 mm) inside the seam allowance; baste. With right sides together, sew the facing to the garment waistline. Grade the seam and understitch.

Preparing Facing
Prepare the facing with interfacing, joining seams and edge-finishing the bottom edge. Serge this edge if using knit fabrics and either serge or turn under ¼" (6 mm) and edgestitch if using a woven fabric. Assemble the pant or skirt, sewing all of the seams and darts and inserting the zipper.

Finishing Facing
Turn the facing to inside of garment and press. To finish, turn under the seam allowances at the center back and slipstitch along the zipper tape. Either stitch-in-the-ditch at the side seams or tack facing to garment at seams and darts. Sew a hook and eye at the closing.

Working with Knits

To emulate the look of quality ready-to-wear garments, knits require special edge and seam finishes. With the help of a serger, they're quick and easy to do, and you'll enjoy professional results every time.

Edge Finishes

With the advent of the serger in the home sewing market, you can now make professional edge and seam finishes for all fabrics. The serger is a natural for sewing with knits and will enable your garment to emulate the look of today's ready-to-wear and to stabilize the entire garment. (Serging is also referred to as overlocking.)

The differential feed feature on the machine can be adjusted to prevent puckers or waving. If the knit fabric has a tendency to curl, edge finishing helps the seams to lie flat.

Because knit fabrics do not ravel, it is not always necessary to edge-finish them. Always test them by stretching them on the cross grain. If the fabric runs or pops, then you definitely need to finish the edges.

Edge finishing may also be accomplished with either a three-thread or four-thread stitch formation. The three-thread option is less bulky.

Serged Edges
Three possible edge finishes (from left): a four-thread formation, a three-thread formation, an edge with no finish.

Serger Seams

For a narrow stretch seam on a lightweight knit, serge your seams with a three-thread stitch formation. Use a four-thread stitch formation on a medium to heavyweight knit; the fourth thread stabilizes the seam. A four-thread seam finishes at approximately ¼" (6 mm), so ⅜" (10 mm) of the seam allowance is cut off by the serger blade. Again, using the differential feed system is extremely helpful.

Serged Seams
Two serger seam finishes (from left): a three-thread formation, a four-thread formation.

NEEDLES FOR KNITS

For knits, the ballpoint with its rounded tip is the needle of choice to avoid breaking fibers and creating holes. Always use the smallest needle size appropriate for your fabric; choose from sizes 70/10, 80/12 and 90/14—the finer the needle, the smaller the number.

Front Bands

Front bands on a coat or jacket create a handsome design detail, give definition to an edge, and prevent sagging and stretching on a knit garment.

ADJUSTING YOUR PATTERN

To create a band when it is not called for in a pattern, first determine the width of the finished band that you desire; for example, 1¼" (3.2 cm). Pin the front pattern piece to the back pattern piece at the shoulder seams. From the edge of the pattern piece, trim away 1¼" (3.2 cm) around the neck and down the front of the pattern. Re-draw the new seamline on the pattern, ⅝" (15 mm) inside the newly-cut edge. Using a soft tape measure standing on its edge, measure from the center back neck curve around the front neckline down to the desired finished hemline, add ⅝" (15 mm), then double the figure.

PREPARING YOUR FABRIC

Using that length, cut a piece of fabric, 1¼" (3.2 cm) wide plus ⅝" (15 mm) times two (3¾"/9.5 cm).

With right sides together, fold band in half lengthwise, serge a ⅝" (15 mm) seam across both ends, and turn ends to the inside. Press the band in half lengthwise with the wrong sides together.

BAND APPLICATION

First sew the shoulder seams and pre-hem the garment.

There are two methods of band application. In the first method, serge both band edges to the right side of the garment front edge in one operation, then press the seam allowances toward the garment.

In the second method, finish one long edge of the band, using the serger, before serging the short ends. Then serge only one edge of the band onto the right side of the garment edge, press the seam allowances toward the band, then topstitch the remaining band edge "in-the-ditch." It may be helpful to baste the band in position before this last step.

Method One
Serge through all three layers with a ⅝" (15 mm) seam, using a four-thread stitch formation.

Method Two, Step One
Serge the unfinished band edge to the garment edge.

Method Two, Step Two
With the free edge of the band now folded and pressed to the underside (covering up the seam), stitch-in-the-ditch on the right side of the garment.

Hem Finishes

Hems in knit garments may be hand-sewn or stitched on the sewing machine or serger. No matter what method you select, allow the garment to hang for at least 24 hours before marking the hem. A hem width of 1¼" (3.2 cm) is fairly standard, but the style of the garment may dictate another choice. In pants for example, a wide, full leg may look better with as much as a 2" (5 cm) hem; and conversely, a tapered leg width may be better suited to a narrow hem of ¾"–1" (20 mm–25 mm).

HAND-SEWN HEMS

The hand-sewn method is the most invisible for quality garments that are dressier and worn less often, since the stitch is less durable than other methods.

MACHINE HEMS

Hems sewn on the sewing machine are slightly more conspicuous and in some cases, even decorative, but are highly durable. They tend to have a sportier look.

Blind Hem

A blind hem stitched on a sewing machine sews fast and looks perfect, especially if you are sewing a considerable length of straight hemming. Fold back the garment, leaving about ¼" (6 mm) of hem exposed. Using the programmed blindstitch on your machine and the special presser foot, position the blade along the fold of the fabric and let the stitch do the work. The needle will sew a few stitches and then swing to the left and just catch a "thread" of the fabric. The result is a durable, concealed hem stitch.

Topstitched Hem

Topstitched hems look best when sewn on the right side of the fabric, and may be done on the sewing machine with a single, double, or triple needle.

Double and triple needles come in various widths and needle sizes. Generally speaking, the finer the fabric, the closer the needles need to be; the heavier the fabric, the wider apart the needles need to be. The wider the needle spread, the more "ridge" is created between the stitching lines. If you do not care for the ridge, you can always sew two lines of topstitching with a single needle. A straight stitch should be adequate, but if more stretch is required, a slight zigzag stitch may help, and not even show, especially if the fabric is textured. Trim the excess fabric close to the stitching on the back side, using your appliqué scissors. Don't worry about raveling.

If the hem tends to wave while sewing, try placing your finger in back of the presser foot and pushing slightly against the foot to help control the stretch.

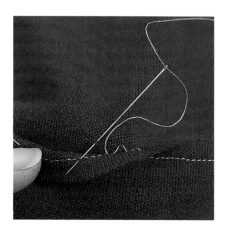

Hand-sewn Hem
Staystitch ¼" (6 mm) from the raw edge, turn up the hem allowance and blindstitch or catchstitch by hand, barely skimming the back side of the fabric.

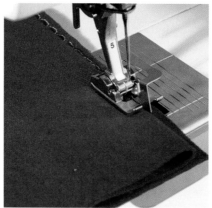

Machine Blind Hem
Fold the garment back on itself to expose about ¼" (6 mm) of hem. Position the presser foot blade next to the fabric fold; the programmed stitch on your machine will do the work.

Double-Needle Topstitched Hem
Sew with a stitch length of 3–3.5 (8 to 10 stitches per inch). On the back side a zigzag stitch is created; trim the fabric close to the stitching line.

SERGED HEMS

As with sewing machine hems, these serged hems offer a sporty look for casual clothes.

The **Blind Hem** stitch is barely visible on the right side of the fabric and overlocks and secures the raw hem edge all in one process.

The **False Blind Hem** has the appearance of a sewn-on band because the seam line appears on the right side of the garment. It's ideal for sweatshirt fabric and leisure wear.

The **Flatlock Hem** is visible on the right side of the garment and is well suited for fine- to medium-weight knits.

THE BLIND STITCH FOOT

Most sergers have an extra accessory called a blind stitch foot. This foot allows you to sew a blind hem, false blind hem or flatlock hem on the serger.

Place the fabric under the foot and adjust the guide plate so that the fold of the fabric is in line with the needle. Feed the fabric so that the fold is always against the guide.

Blind Hem
Use a blind stitch foot (see upper right photo) and fold fabric as shown. Using a three-thread overlock and the right-hand needle, set the stitch length to 4 and the cutting width to 2. Reduce the needle thread tension. After stitching is completed, open out the fabric and press lightly on the wrong side.

False Blind Hem
Prepare the hem as in the blind-hem technique, and place fabric under the presser foot. Adjust the guide to the right so that the needle just pierces the fold. Use a three-thread overlock, 2.5 stitch length and a cutting width of 2, with normal tension. After sewing, press hem flat.

Flatlock Hem
Set your serger to a stitch length of 3–4 and a cutting width of 2. The upper looper should have very little tension (practically zero), the lower looper almost full tension, and the needle thread no tension. After stitching a test sample, gently pull the seam apart and press. If the seam does not flatten out, thread the right needle thread around the left needle thread tension dial and adjust it to zero.

CHAPTER 5

Victor Costa

Victor Costa's name is synonymous with the glamour and wealth of international celebrities—a list of his clientele reads like a "Who's Who" of fashion. But unlike many well-known fashion designers, Costa does not focus his attention solely on the elite. He also designs with the goal of dressing the everyday woman without cutting into her tight budget. His philosophy is to give a customer the latest styles at a price she can afford.

Nowhere is this concept more important than in bridal wear. One of the most exciting sewing projects a woman can undertake is the creation of a formal wedding gown. Here are expert tips to show you how to execute a fabulous gown—from a perfect fit, to working with lace, to finishing with impeccable details.

Designing for Special Occasions

Creating your own wedding gown can be one of the most rewarding sewing experiences of your life. It provides you an opportunity to showcase your own mood, message and image through pattern and fabric selection in this once-in-a-lifetime garment.

The Designer at Work

When Costa designs, he keeps two women in mind: the older woman who wants to look glamorous, yet needs to strategically camouflage her neck and upper arms, and the younger woman who can successfully wear the bolder, barer fashions. He tailors his designs to conceal women's imperfections such as heavy hips or untoned arms; his goal is to flatter all women's figures. Costa believes that, after establishing themselves in a man's world, women of the '90s want to redeem and flaunt their feminine qualities. Costa's aim is to design dresses that are comfortable, flattering, timeless and affordable for women in every size and age group.

Although Costa is known as the "copy artist" of the fashion world—reproducing top designers' dresses and making them affordable—he is well admired and respected by his colleagues. Costa's training—at New York City's Pratt Institute and Ecole de la Chambre Syndicale de la Couture Parisienne in Paris—helped him to become a household name in the fashion world. His first job after schooling was with a bridal design firm; perhaps that is where his desire to create opulent-looking fashion of great drama was first nurtured.

Costa's natural talent and eye for designs enable him to produce five clothing collections, eighty new designs and travel to Europe six times—every year! The Victor Costa label is a diverse one, embracing not only his famous ready-to-wear collections, but also his suit collection—Tailleur—and Victor Costa Bridal, which includes bridal, bridesmaid and debutante designs. Many famous wedding dresses have involved his custom touch, including one worn by the daughter of John Fairchild, publisher of *Women's Wear Daily*.

Costa feels a kinship with home sewers. "Home sewers have a very creative job to do," he says. "They have to find the fabrics to suit the designs. I encourage the home sewer to use her imagination...to take a plain, dollar-a-yard lace and embroider it with silk floss, crystal or flowers."

Personalizing Your Gown

The bodice of a wedding gown is often identified as "close fitting" in the caption on the back of a pattern envelope. This term indicates there is less design ease than in other garments. To achieve the very close fit of a strapless bodice, you will find body-defining darts, princess seaming and little or no ease at the bustline. With the close-to-the-body shape, you may need to re-evaluate the pattern size you are buying.

MEASURING YOURSELF

Begin your pattern size checkup by accurately measuring your bust, waist and hips. Use your bust measurement to determine the correct pattern size to buy. If there is a difference of over 2" (5 cm) between your bust and chest measurements, use your chest measurement to choose your pattern size. Patterns are designed for a B cup, so you can use the bust measurement if you are an A or B cup. If you are a C cup or larger, you will need to use the chest measurement instead.

The chest measurement affects the critical fit areas through your chest, upper back and shoulders. It is easier to alter the bust area than the chest and shoulder areas. If you use your chest measurement to buy your pattern size, you will need to make a cup adjustment to ensure that the garment fits you properly.

Length measurements are also crucial. Be sure to take the following measurements: back waist length (the measurement from the prominent bone at the base of your neck to your waist), the length from your waist to your hip, and the total length from your waistline to your desired finished length.

ADJUSTING THE PATTERN

To begin your adjustment procedure, separate the pattern pieces, leaving margins along edges. Press out wrinkles with a warm, dry iron. Observe the cutting lines for the different sizes in a multisized pattern. The outside line is not always the largest size, especially at the neckline and armhole.

Look at the valuable fit information on your pattern tissue. You will find three fit guidelines. Usually, a symbol marks the bust point. Near this symbol is the finished garment measurement for the bust area for that specific design. A "BEFORE YOU CUT" instruction tells you how much more the pattern measures than the body measurement, for that style. To ensure

that your finished garment will have the same amount of ease the designer intended, compare your bust measurement with the pattern body measurement. Then subtract the pattern body measurement from the printed measurement at the bust point on the pattern. This will give you the ease at the bustline. Also subtract your own bust measurement from the printed measurement at the bustline. If the ease measurements (plus or minus) are not identical, make the necessary pattern adjustments.

Flat pattern adjustments allow you to make your pattern statistically accurate, but they cannot perfectly accommodate your unique figure—your posture, weight and bone structure. These significant personal alterations must be worked out in fittings: first with pattern pieces, second with a muslin, and finally with the garment.

Most bridal patterns offer one style with several versions. This is the same style as the gown on the previous page, but in a bridesmaid's version.

MAKING A MUSLIN

For designs that fit extremely close to the body and demand a perfect fit, it is essential to make a sample garment before cutting your fabric. This sample garment is called a "muslin," as is the fabric commonly used in its construction. Actually, the fabric used can range from heavy-weight muslin to gingham. The aim is to substitute a heavy-weight, on-grain fabric for a heavy-weight fashion fabric and a lightweight, on-grain fabric for a delicate fashion fabric. You may substitute non-woven pattern tracing material for lace, which has no grain. To eliminate shrinkage, steam-press all materials before cutting.

Make a muslin with the adjusted pattern pieces. Cut out, allowing 1" (25 mm) seam allowances on shoulder and lengthwise seams. Using a tracing wheel and dressmaker's tracing paper, trace all seamlines and symbols on both sides so changes will be obvious. Mark lengthwise and crosswise grains on the right side of the fabric. Staystitch top (or neckline) edge, armholes and waist. Construct garment, using machine basting for easier fitting changes.

Besides allowing you to check pattern adjustments and perfect the fit, making a muslin gives you a chance to analyze how the overall style flatters you, to check scale and placement of details, to test how the garment hangs, and to assess the construction procedures. This inexpensive prototype is well worth the time and effort spent before cutting into elegant and expensive fabric. As you will see, specialty seam treatments for lace will make fit alterations difficult at a later stage.

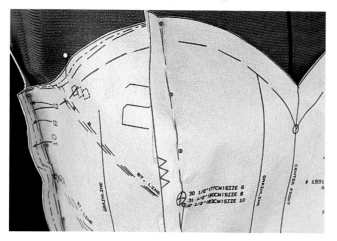

Pin-fitting the Pattern
After adjusting your pattern pieces for fit, blend the interrupted edges with a smooth line, then trim away all excess margins from the pattern. Draw seamlines on the pattern pieces, pin together and "try on" your pin-fitted pattern, wearing the shoes and undergarments that will be worn with the gown. Make changes on the pattern pieces where necessary.

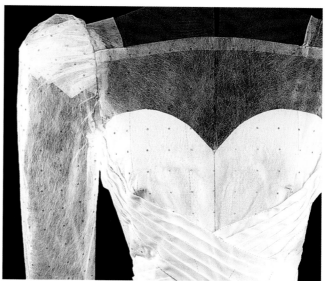

Fitting the Muslin
Try on muslin, wearing shoes and undergarments to be worn with the gown. After adding ease or eliminating excess fabric, transfer all adjustments onto the pattern pieces and blend the edges.

FITTING CHECKLIST

1. The neckline should rest smoothly against the body, without wrinkles or gaps.
2. The shoulder seam should run across the top of the shoulder at a slope that does not pull or wrinkle.
3. The armhole seam should be comfortable and without strain. It should be about 1" (25 mm) below the armpit, continue around the natural creases created between the body and arm, and rest smoothly on top of the shoulder bone without puckering.
4. The sleeve cap should not ripple in front or back.
5. The length of the sleeve should be comfortable, and the sleeve should have a slightly eased area around the elbow.
6. The bust shaping should fall at the fullest part of the bust.
7. The back should be comfortable without pulling or straining.
8. The midriff area should not strain with wrinkles.
9. The waist should be comfortable and allow a smooth transition between midriff and skirt.
10. The skirt should not strain across the hips.
11. The hem should be a flattering length.

Sewing with Lace

Laces are perennial favorites for wedding gowns. Although many sewers are apprehensive about working with lace, you will be delighted to discover that working with lace need not be anxiety-producing because it eliminates the problem of raveling and having to work with the straight grain of fabric. And the results are so rewarding!

Lace Characteristics

Formal laces are intricately decorative and often have a fancy surface treatment. Many have a net or mesh background with repeated motifs and finished, scalloped borders. Good quality laces are delicate and may be enriched by hand or machine, with cord, ribbon, sequins, pearls or beads.

The net or mesh construction allows you to disregard the grainline and work creatively with the scallops and motifs. Often these laces are relatively narrow and used for panels, trimming and appliqué, though they may work beautifully into a bodice or sleeve.

Allover lace, made entirely by machine, has repeated motifs throughout the yardage, but not necessarily a scallop treatment along the edges; some motifs are repetitive enough to be cut into strips for a decorative edge treatment. Often narrow matching lace trim is available.

Planning Your Gown

You may choose to use lace for an entire gown or just a portion of it. When buying lace, check pattern yardage and fabric cutting layouts—lace with a one-way design requiring a nap layout may not be suitable or may require extra yardage. Plan how you can best use a selected lace before making a purchase. Let the motifs, lace weight and density guide you in creating a look. The main concern is the design in the lace and its direction, because lace may be cut lengthwise, crosswise or favoring an edge.

Look carefully at the motifs to determine if portions may be used as an edge treatment, eliminating facing or hem. You may finish outer edges with scalloped borders, appliquéd trim, or a binding of net or sheer tricot.

Depending on the type and weight of lace you select, you will have to decide whether and how to line your gown. Some of the most beautiful lace gowns have no inner supporting fabrics. Consider only underlinings or "under fabrics" that will not detract from the appearance of your lace. Underlining or backing works best on sheer or openwork lace; in a matching or contrasting color, it can add another dimension to your gown as well as comfort and support.

Some laces are both delicate and scratchy, and your wedding-day comfort should be a factor. To give nearly invisible body and support, back fragile lace with net or tulle. Backing can be sheer or opaque; try satin, taffeta, organdy, crepe, marquisette or nude tricot to create your special effect.

If working with a light-colored lace, cover cutting surface with a smooth, dark cloth. Spread lace in a single layer over covered surface. Place complete pattern pieces over lace. Balance motifs on either side of the gown's center front and back, or place motifs at the centers.

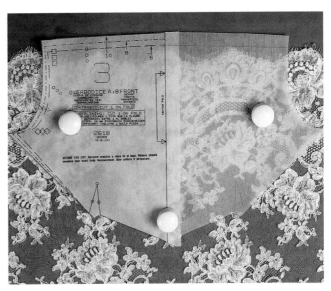

Laying out Lace with Usable Motifs
Fix pattern pieces in place with weights or fine glass-headed silk pins. Cut with sharp dressmaker's shears.

Cutting Lace

When planning to appliqué seams, allow for complete motif outlines on edges so these can be matched and lapped at the seamlines. Carefully plan and arrange your work as you would a plaid; balance motifs in a pleasing manner and plot designs of adjoining pieces. Weight or pin pieces in place when satisfied that all pieces will blend together.

Reimbroidered lace (in which a cord outlines individual floral motifs) merits extra thought. Although the general statement that lace does not ravel holds true, you will be more pleased with the results if you avoid cutting into the cord as much as possible to keep the outlines intact. This will also make your appliqué work easier to sew.

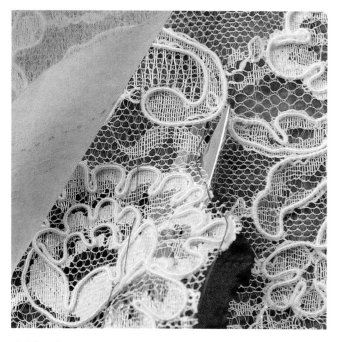

Cutting Lace
For easy cutting of the lapped seam, thread-trace the motif outline outside the seamline. In another thread color, trace along the seamline. Cut outside the extended motifs of the lapped edge and cut the normal ⅝" (15 mm) seam allowance (or wider for a larger design) on the underlap edge. Use this method only after you are certain no more fitting is needed.

Construction Pointers for Lace

PRESSING

Test-press on lace fabric scraps before pressing the cut-out pieces and the constructed gown. Use a press pad or Turkish towel under lace to avoid flattening the design. Place lace right side down, then steam. Check and follow instructions on the hang tag or bolt end of the lace you purchased. Some embellishments may be damaged in the steaming process. A see-through press cloth protects the fabric and prevents the iron from catching in the lace.

NEEDLES AND THREAD

Using scraps, experiment with needle size and thread. Using a new size 12/80 universal needle, thread the machine with cotton or polyester thread. To prevent puckering, hold fabric firmly in front and back while machine stitching; do not pull. Slowly sew with a stitch length of 2.5 (12 stitches per inch). Change needle and thread combinations, stitch length, and thread tension until you achieve the desired effect. Try a larger, sharper needle when sewing re-embroidered lace that has pearls, sequins and beads. Do not sew directly over these embellishments; remove those on the stitching line.

SPECIAL CONSIDERATIONS

If the presser foot catches in the lace, wrap tape around the front of the foot, or switch to a jeans or a roller foot. If lace continues to get caught on the foot, sew with strips of tissue paper or Solvy® (a transparent stabilizer) under the foot. If lace gets drawn down into the needle hole, switch to the straight-stitch plate or place strips of tissue paper under the fabric as you sew.

Traditional methods of seam and dart construction are fine for opaque, backed or bonded laces. These seams can be adjusted in the final fitting. Structural seams in fragile laces are handled with double-stitched or serged seams. These seams are difficult to alter.

Joining Thread-traced Seam
Overlap the seamlines along the thread-tracing lines, basting the overlapped motif extensions to the adjoining piece. Using a contrasting thread, mark symbols with tailor's tacks. Clipping notches is not necessary.

Trimming a Lapped Seam
After stitching motif in place, trim "whiskers" on top. On the inside, trim away underlap close to the stitching. A dart may be handled similarly by clipping and overlapping.

Stitching a Lapped Seam
Appliqué the motif edge to the underlapped piece with tiny whipstitches or zigzag stitches. Check your machine manual for the specific feet and stitch widths/lengths to use.

Appliquéing Lace Trim

PLANNING THE APPLIQUÉ

Sometimes you cannot position and cut pattern pieces to form a scalloped lace edge where you would like—around a curved neckline, sleeve or hem. In that case, appliqué a lace border to the edge. Use a strip of purchased lace trim, a line of motifs cut from a scalloped border on lace yardage, or a repeated pattern of motifs cut from the interior of lace yardage. Place the lace strip over an edge that needs to be finished or is already hemmed. For a pleasing effect, take care to balance your work, placing small motifs on small sections, such as collars and cuffs, and larger motifs on larger sections, such as the skirt.

Shaping Lace Appliqué
Overlap appliqué motif edges so they form a continuous pattern. For especially curved edges, try steam pressing or clip between motifs so the strip will lie flat; pin and baste.

ARRANGING THE APPLIQUÉ

To complete a scalloped border similar to the one on our gown, cut a large triangular piece from the scalloped edge of a lace galloon, to fit the lower front edge of the skirt. Place the scalloped border of this piece over the finished front skirt hem. Hand or machine-stitch close to the upper edge of the lace.

For the remainder of the hem trim, cut a scalloped border, favoring the motifs. Pin to the finished hem of the skirt back, placing inner edge of scallops along entire lower edge with ends overlapping side edges of front appliqué, making motif design continuous as far as possible. Sew upper edge of scallops invisibly and securely in place by hand. Sew ends to skirt front appliqué invisibly and securely by hand, keeping garment free.

To finish the upper edge of the large appliqué on the front panel, position separate motifs cut from the remainder of the lace to form a pleasing and continuous lace design. Sew motifs invisibly and securely in place by hand.

Trimming Lace Appliqué
Appliqué inner edge to garment using machine zigzag or hand whipstitches. Trim fabric close to the zigzag or whipstitches, exposing decorative edge of appliqué.

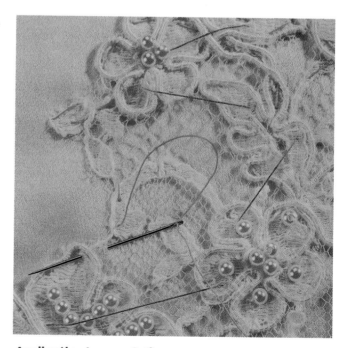

Appliquéing Lace on Satin
Pin wrong side of appliqué to right side of satin. Baste in place. Sew, using small hand stitches along the border and inside the motif, taking care not to pucker lace or satin. If lace lends itself, machine-stitch close to cut edge, using a narrow zigzag or straight stitch.

Beautiful Finishes

Just as you want every detail of your wedding day to be perfect, you also want every added touch on your wedding gown to be flawless. It pays to spend a little extra time and thought on these details, because—some day—your gown may be an heirloom!

Closure Options

The most frequently used closures on wedding gowns are buttons and loops or zippers, but of course you may consider other treatments. Underlined, backed, and medium- to heavy-weight laces can usually support any closure. Use zippers for underlined, backed or opaque laces only. Some laces lend themselves to buttonholes or loops and buttons, or bound edges that extend into ties. Evaluate the delicacy of your lace, weight of the closures, and design of the gown before proceeding. Be sure your lace can withstand the handling involved; consider reinforcing the opening with a strip of tulle before attaching closures. On loosely-fitted garments, clear snaps offer an alternative to a zipper. Our sample gown includes a zipper application in satin and then a loop and button treatment in the lace, which has been backed with netting.

BUTTON AND LOOP CLOSURES

Button and loop closures are a traditional, favorite touch on bridal gowns, lending a formal and refined look. Remember that during a wedding ceremony many eyes will be on the back of your gown! Evaluate which style of loops would best suit your gown. A continuous length of cording made of silk or a compatible fabric works well on gowns of medium- to heavy-weight fabric. Tape with elasticized loops works well on delicate laces, and is easier to apply.

Self-fabric Loops
If creating your own loops, first sew $^3/_8$" (10 mm) buttons along right side, $^1/_2$" (13 mm) apart and $^1/_8$" (3 mm) from the edge. Position left back edge alongside and indicate markings for loops, $^1/_4$" (6 mm) above and $^1/_4$" (6 mm) below the button placement. Sew a small portion of the cording securely in place at the top marking. Tack cording to opening edge at remaining markings, forming even loops which accommodate your button. Sew the cut end of the last loop securely and invisibly in place.

Elastic Loop Tape
Pin $^1/_8$" (3 mm) inside the left back edge (with loops extending beyond edge), then secure with prickstitches. Mark button placement opposite loops on right back; sew small buttons $^1/_8$" (3 mm) from edge.

ZIPPER CLOSURE

Fold lining back along center back so it will not interfere with zipper application. Remove any pearls, beads or sequins that are on the line of stitching. Check that the zipper is the correct length; the zipper should measure $^1/_4$" (6 mm) less than the basted opening to allow for a hook and eye. Make a new zipper stop if a shorter zipper is required.

For prickstitches, bring needle up through all thicknesses to the right (top) side. Take a stitch backwards a distance of only one or two threads, forming a tiny surface stitch. Bring the needle up again a scant $^1/_4$" (6 mm) from the first stitch.

Zipper Placement
Open zipper; place face down on extended seam allowance, placing zipper stop $^1/_4$" (6 mm) below lower marking and zipper teeth on seamline. Baste in center of zipper tape on one side, catching seam allowance only.

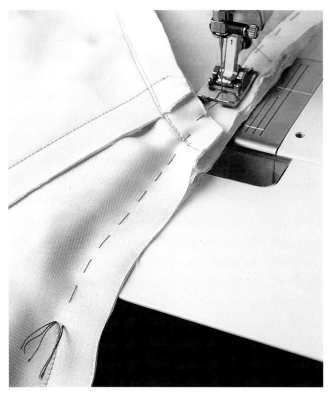

Basting Center Back
Baste opening edges of gown together along seamline above the marking that indicates the lower end of the zipper, keeping any skirt pleats and lace free. (Because of the many layers, this sample is basted by hand first.)

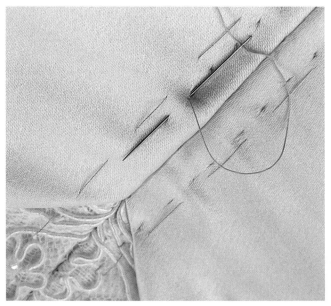

Prickstitching the Zipper
Close zipper; turn pull tab up. Spread garment flat. Baste a scant $^1/_4$" (6 mm) from zipper teeth and across lower edge, checking from inside to outside that the zipper is centered over the seam. On outside, sew by hand with a prickstitch along basting, through all thicknesses. Remove basting once zipper is secured.

FINISHING THE WAIST

To eliminate pressure on the zipper, add a ribbon at the waistline. Cut a 1" (25 mm) wide grosgrain ribbon the length of the pattern waist plus 1¹/₂" (3.8 cm) for each end. Turn under ¹/₂" (13 mm), then turn under ¹/₄" (6 mm) on raw edges. Whipstitch to hold. On the inside of the gown, pin the ribbon to the bodice lining, centering over the waistline. Tack at seams, leaving opening at center back. Sew hook(s) and eye(s) to ribbon ends.

Slipstitching the Lining

Turn bodice lining down (wrong sides of bodice and lining together). Turn under seam allowance on center back edges of lining to clear zipper teeth; lightly press. On overbodice lace, sew a ⁵/₈" (15 mm) narrow hem by hand along the center back opening. Slipstitch pressed edges of lining to bodice along zipper tape and waist seam. When sewing, take care to slide the needle carefully through the folded edge and pick up just a single thread of underneath fabric.

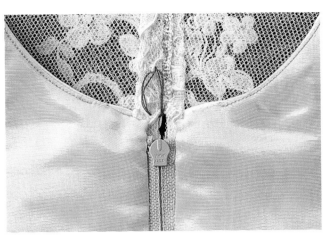

Finishing the Inside Zipper Edge
Slipstitch folded hem of lace above zipper. Slipstitch folded edge of lining to zipper tape.

HEMMING THE GOWN

"Horsehair"—a lightweight, almost-transparent nylon braid—gives hemlines a crisp, stiff edge, and offers a professional finish. It comes in several widths; this model features 1" (25 mm)-wide horsehair. Establish finished length of gown and trim hem, allowing twice the width of the horsehair as hem width.

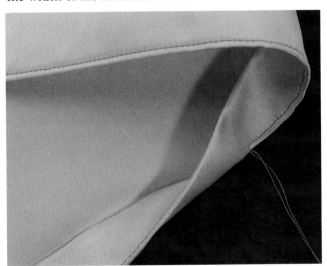

Horsehair Braid
Along the lower edge of skirt, turn fabric under the same width as the horsehair braid. Press, easing in fullness. Unfold pressed edge and pin horsehair braid to outside along crease, lapping ends at center back. Stitch ends, keeping gown free; trim close to stitching. Stitch close to edge of horsehair, then turn it to inside of skirt along stitching. Turn in and press lower edge of gown again to conceal horsehair (this prevents snagging of stockings and catching along carpeting). Edgestitch close to the fold, through all thicknesses. Hand-tack to seams if necessary.

CHAPTER 6

Claude Montana

Claude Montana's clothes have a reputation for being avant-garde yet very sophisticated, and have always pointed towards the fashion trends to come. His designs have the feeling of the future, yet are grounded in the moment, and Montana's clothing has amazing staying power. His early designs look current twenty years later.

Scrutiny of Montana's "forward" designs reveals that, ironically, he honors traditional tailoring techniques and employs them to achieve his sculptural creations. Now you, too, can learn these time-tested methods, whether your desire is to master working with gabardine, executing a flawless tailored collar or venturing into the exciting world of real and synthetic leathers.

The Master Tailor

Montana's use of gabardine provides a canvas for clean, almost severe details. The stand-up collar, double welt pocket, placket and button insets become dramatic carved lines when sewn in a hard-surfaced fabric.

The Designer at Work

Claude Montana has always had a strong sense of his own vision of clothing design. His clothes have a look, an identifiable style, a voice that is uniquely his own. A Frenchman, he began his career at twenty in London during the height of swinging Carnaby Street, designing extravagant *papier mâché* jewelry.

When Montana returned to Paris he discovered a passion for leather and went to school to study it. He emerged from his training with a fresh feeling for the way the women and men of his generation wanted to look and feel.

Montana has created collections for the finest French ready-to-wear or *prêt-à-porter* since 1979 when he started his own company with an enthusiastic team which still closely surrounds him today. He continues to support new talent, giving his time to fashion design schools and hiring students as apprentices—a coveted position among aspiring designers.

In 1990, Montana joined the House of Lanvin to create their Haute Couture collections which brought him the Gold Thimble (Dè d'Or), the highest honor in the French fashion field.

Montana designs a men's line, a premier women's line, and recently a "bridge" (more affordable) line called State of Claude Montana.

He also has fragrances for men and women for which he has received several awards.

For anyone with an appreciation of fabric, fashion or design, it is pure inspiration to see, touch, and try on Montana's premier line of clothing. His more outrageous designs may get photographed in magazines and newspapers, but most of his clothes are designed to be worn in the real world with pleasure and confidence.

Montana's Favored Fabrics

Montana was one of the first designers to elevate the use of leather to high fashion. Over the years, Montana's fascination with leather as a material has never ceased and he continues to use it throughout his collections. Montana uses leather as a master tailor uses fine fabrics. All-leather garments appear in nearly every one of his collections, styled as classics with a twist or as pull-out-all-the-stops high fashion. He frequently uses leather in combination with wool for collars, cuffs, pocket detailing, piping and bound buttonholes. Consider using real leather or the new synthetic Ultraleather® for a touch of sophisticated luxury on your own Claude Montana-inspired garments.

Montana also favors wool with a firm finish, and gabardine is one of his mainstays. He uses this crisp fabric like a sculptor, shaping his garments with seams and darts so a woman's figure is enhanced and dramatized. Gabardine also lends itself beautifully to the angular lines of the menswear look for women.

The sculptural lines of a Montana suit attest to his art form—using fabric to create shape. Upon closer observation, notice the beautifully curved lines of the jacket, with the dart and pocket combining as one design element.

Mastering Gabardine

Gabardine is the designer's choice for sophisticated, highly tailored styles that require crispness, yet need good drape. Here are some tricks of the trade.

Gabardine's Characteristics

Wool gabardine or any firmly woven worsted fabric is two-dimensional, flat and wrinkle resistant, smooth and cool to the touch. Fluid, flowing and seductive to touch, its very nature makes the fabric so attractive but can also cause frustration in sewing and pressing. In European men's custom tailoring shops it is common to have one or two master tailors who specialize in all the gabardine work.

Select styles and details carefully. For first-time success, choose raglan or dropped sleeves, band collar or collarless neckline, and a relaxed fit. Gabardine is difficult to ease without looking puckered, so avoid set-in sleeves and notched collar construction unless you are an advanced sewer. Light colors are more forgiving than dark in pressing. Be willing to test on fabric scraps until you are satisfied with the results. Have your fabric preshrunk at the cleaners, for even such a firm fabric can shrink during pressing.

Finishing seams with rayon seam binding works well (see Chapter 2). Gabardine does not always require a lining, but rayon bemberg and silk crepe de Chine are compatible lining fabrics. If lining a gabardine garment, it is not necessary to finish the seams. Serging may "strike through" (show when pressed). If serging an edge on an unlined gabardine garment, use a very fine thread. Woolly nylon used on the loopers gives a soft, velvety finish.

When sewing gabardine, use a slightly shorter stitch length than usual—about 2 (14 stitches per inch)—and a size 12/80 universal needle.

PRESSING TOOLS FOR GABARDINE

The secret to creating great-looking gabardine garments lies in assembling a few important tools and fine-tuning your pressing techniques. Pressing makes the crucial difference in the success of a professional finish. You will need the following tools:

• The **clapper,** made of hardwood to absorb heat and steam, flattens seams and edges with its weight while the fabric is cooling. This sets the press.

• The **tailor's ham,** with a curved surface covered with cotton on one side, wool on the other, is used for pressing shaped areas. Use the cotton side for high temperatures. Press wool against the wool side to hold steam, minimizing shine. A ham holder to keep the ham stable is a nice extra.

• **Press cloths** provide a protective layer between the iron and fabric. Use a see-through press cloth for fusing thin, fine fabrics and when you need to see your work. Heavy cotton drill holds heat and moisture for pressing heavy fabric and gives a crisp edge when used with the clapper. A scrap of wool or self fabric is excellent—wool responds well next to wool, holds steam and moisture, and prevents shine and "strike-through"—the imprint of a seam or edge.

• Use a **tailor's brush,** with densely packed, but soft, brass bristles, to lightly rough up an area that may have been overpressed and has become shiny.

• The wooden, contoured **press board** has curved and flat surfaces for pressing open enclosed seams and flattening detail areas—nothing flattens as well as wood against wool.

These tools are the secret to a beautifully crafted wool gabardine garment that looks like the designer original. There are additional pressing tools, but these are a good start.

Pressing Gabardine

White vinegar helps "set" a press and prevents shine. Mix 3–4 tablespoons of white vinegar per cup of water. Put a few tablespoons of vinegar-water in a plant mister or sponge directly on fabric, but always test first. Use it directly over a seam on the wrong side while pressing. No odor remains.

Pretest your fabric to see what iron temperature scorches the fabric or makes it shine. Can you press this fabric on the right side? Which press cloth works best? How much pressure or pounding should you use with the clapper? Will white vinegar be necessary?

Press each seam and dart flat, as sewn, to meld (blend) the stitches and ease the thread. While fabric is still warm, finger-press the seam open, then press it open and straight, using the clapper and allowing fabric to cool before moving. Use a press-and-lift motion with the iron and clapper, overlapping to avoid marks.

It may be necessary to overpress to achieve the desired degree of flatness. Test removing a shine, using the tailor's brush or a scrap of wool dampened with white vinegar to rough up the surface a bit, camouflaging the overpressing. Be careful—there is a point beyond which the wool is pressed flat, but cannot be revitalized. Master tailors refer to it as "killing" the wool.

To avoid seam imprint, try pressing seams open on the point presser or seam roll. "Erase" seam imprint on the right side by pressing under the seam on the wrong side with the tip of the iron. Finish by slipping strips of butcher or brown paper beneath seams. Press, then clap. With particularly stubborn fabrics, press seams open using the stick attachment on the multipress sleeve board.

Topstitching and edgestitching are often the best way to keep "a press" in position.

Using the Clapper, Ham and Press Board
Use the clapper each time you press: when pressing darts, opening seams, flattening edges. Press a small section at a time, pounding, holding or setting the clapper over the area until fabric cools. Press curved seams and darts over the ham, using the clapper. The clapper point presser has a point presser built-in—handy for straight seams. Use the contoured press board to open straight or curved narrow, trimmed seams.

THE BENEFITS OF USING SILK THREAD

Silk thread is the perfect choice for hand basting, securing hems, delicate hand tacking or stitching on the inside of a garment. It is ideal for basting because it does not leave a permanent mark or impression on the fabric when pressed. It is easy to remove after topstitching over it. Because of silk's unique characteristics, it takes on the color of the fabric that it's stitched on, so that an exact color match is not necessary. Silk thread, with its smooth and beautiful surface, does not tangle as much as other threads.

Enclosed Seams

Carefully executed enclosed seams result in a garment with flat straight edges and smooth curves that curve slightly to the inside. Use these techniques on all fabrics for professional results. Success depends on accurate stitching, even trimming or grading, hand-basting and meticulous pressing at each step.

Enclosed seams on facings and collars should be graded or layered with the wider side against the right side of the garment, acting as a pad. Grade the narrow layer first, NEVER narrower than a generous $1/8$" (3 mm). Allow more for fabrics which fray. Grade the second layer $1/8$" (3 mm) wider than the first and so on. Tip: Long-bladed shears work best for long seams.

Pressing the Enclosed Seam
Press the graded enclosed seam flat as sewn. Press open, using a point presser or contoured pressing board. Use the point to reach into corners. Position on curved edges as needed. Working from the wrong side, roll (or favor) the seam edge to the underside $1/8$" (3 mm) and hand-baste in position, using silk thread and a diagonal basting stitch. Press edge flat with iron, using clapper and working in sections, allowing each section to cool before proceeding.

Topstitching and Edgestitching

Decorative and functional, topstitching can be the perfect solution to hold seams, edges, and hems in place. Plan topstitching carefully to harmonize with the style, fabric and construction. Keep your eye on ready-to-wear for topstitching details to incorporate into your sewing. Experiment with the distance from the edge, as well as with various threads and needles. Use thick, coarse thread to make the stitching stand out. Certain polyester and silk buttonhole twist threads are designed for this purpose. Achieve a similar effect with two spools of all-purpose thread threaded through the same tension and one needle.

Use a topstitching needle with these heavier threads. Topstitching needles come in the same sizes as all machine needles, but have a longer eye to accommodate the thread and prevent fraying or skipped stitches. Use the same needle size as you have used to sew the garment (or one larger). Patterns give guidelines for determining the distance from the edge, but experiment. Fine, firmly woven fabrics look best when sewn with smaller stitches and finer thread. Heavy-weight fabrics demand longer stitches and stitching farther from the finished edge. Hint: Don't try to force the presser foot too close to the edge—especially with heavy fabrics and wider seams beneath. The best proportion is usually an easy-to-sew wider width.

Design topstitching carefully. Ask these questions: What is the best distance from the edge? What is the ideal needle, size, stitch length and thread? How many rows of stitching? Make practice samples.

Edgestitching (stitching just next to a finished edge) works best with flat, thin edges on light- to medium-weight fabrics. The edgestitching foot makes it easy to sew straight and true along an edge.

SEWING A DART IN GABARDINE

Because gabardine is not as forgiving as more loosely woven fabric, a dart must be sewn perfectly to avoid a pucker at the end. Transfer the marking with tailor's tacks to preserve the tissue pattern. Mark the sewing lines with a chalk marker, and pin these lines together accurately. Machine-stitch from the wide end to the point, using stitch length 2 (14 stitches per inch). For the last $1/2$" (13 mm) of the dart, reduce the stitch length to 1 (18 stitches per inch) to avoid tying a knot or backstitching.

Tailoring Collars

An expertly tailored collar not only takes the shape the designer intended, but will hold its shape for the life of the garment. Follow these steps to unlock the secrets of this inside story.

Custom Tailoring the Undercollar

This classic old-world method is time-consuming but gratifying and with it you will gain an understanding and appreciation of a technique used only in the most expensive clothing today. Hand tailoring is used for women's couture suits selling in the $8,000–$20,000 range, and for men in "bespoke" (sewn one at a time to an individual's measurements) suits. Custom tailoring is best suited to textured woolens: tweeds, medium to heavy-weight wool crepe. You'll have to take more care with gabardine, flannel or hard-surfaced fabrics which do not respond well to hand-sewn pad stitching because it can show through.

The undercollar on a coat or jacket determines the shape and supports the upper collar. The "roll line," indicated on the undercollar pattern piece, divides the area that lies next to the neck—the "stand"—from the outer visible portion—the "fall." Interface both under-collar and upper collar. Fusible tricot makes the perfect choice for upper collar and facing. This keeps this highly visible area smooth, flat and stable and makes it compatible with the shaped areas of the garment front and undercollar.

Traditional hand-shaping with hair canvas and hand-stitching sculpts lasting shape into the undercollar. Made of a blend of wool and goat hair, sometimes rayon or cotton, hair canvas is a sew-in interfacing for tailor-ing. Cut undercollar and hair canvas on the bias with a seam at center back. Transfer center back seamline and roll line to canvas with tracing wheel and paper.

HAND STITCHES FOR TAILORED COLLARS

Use a short fine needle with silk or smooth polyester thread. Make horizontal stitches from right to left, parallel to each other, forming diagonal threads on the top side. There are two stitches, made in the same way, one long (basting) and one short (padstitching).

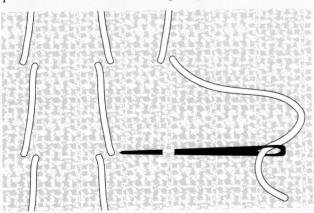

Diagonal Basting
For diagonal basting, make long (1/2"–1"/13 mm–25 mm) stitches. Do not pull thread tight; it should lie flat and smooth. Use diagonal basting in the final pressing of the edges of collars, facings and enclosed seams.

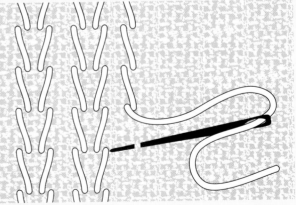

Padstitching
Take small (scant 1/8"/3 mm), short (1/4"–1/2"/6 mm–13 mm apart) stitches. Sew through interfacing, catching only a thread of the gar-ment. Padstitching should be invisible from the outside. End pad-stitching 1/8" (3 mm) from seamlines so canvas can be trimmed later in construction.

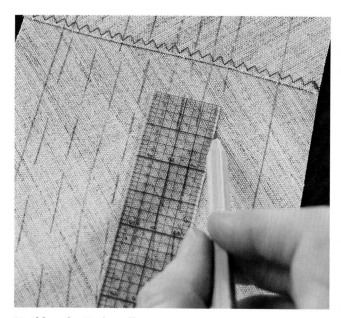

Marking the Undercollar

Sew center back seam on undercollar, trim to $^3/8$" (10 mm), press and pound. Lap seam on hair canvas, trim allowances close ($^1/8$"/3 mm) to stitching. Mark padstitching lines on hair canvas. Using a soft lead pencil, mark parallel lines radiating out from the roll line at $^1/4$" (6 mm) intervals in the stand, $^3/8$" (10 mm) intervals in the outer collar.

Shaping the Padstitched Collar

Use this technique for both hand-tailored and fusible methods. Set the roll line: position undercollar as collar will be worn, and shape along roll line. Pin to ham. Steam, holding iron away from fabric. Cool to set.

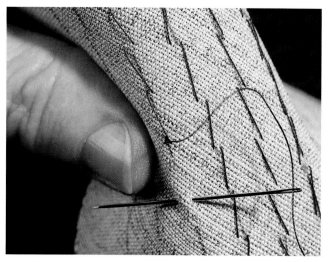

Padstitching Canvas to Collar

Attach canvas to collar at roll line only using a running basting stitch. Beginning at roll line, padstitch back and forth: use $^1/4$" (6 mm) stitches in the stand, $^3/8$"–$^1/2$" (10 mm–13 mm) stitches in the fall. Curve fabric over fingers, and sew in the shape of the curve.

Fusible Undercollar Shaping

Quick and simple, using fusible interfacings is the best way to tailor gabardine and hard-surfaced fabrics, as well as soft and textured fabrics. Variations of this technique are common in ready-to-wear. Tailoring with fusibles is appropriate for all sewing skill levels, beginners to advanced.

Pre-shrink fusibles by dipping in hot tap water and air drying. Test a variety of interfacings with each project, using scraps leftover after cutting. Fusibles can change the character of a fabric, making it crisper or maintaining the drape. Assemble a variety of interfacings with proven success: fusible tricot, Sof Knit®, weft insertion (Suit Shape®, Whisper Weft®), Pellon Sof Shape®. It is acceptable to use a combination of different interfacings on one garment.

INTERFACING THE UPPER COLLAR AND FRONT FACING

Whether you hand-tailor or fuse the undercollar, always interface the upper collar and front facing with fusible tricot or Sof Knit. This balances the weight of both layers of fabric and assures a smooth, flat lapel. Do not trim away the interfacing seam allowance; the tiny amount remaining after grading adds stability but little bulk. After fusing, reposition pattern pieces to add markings to interfacing.

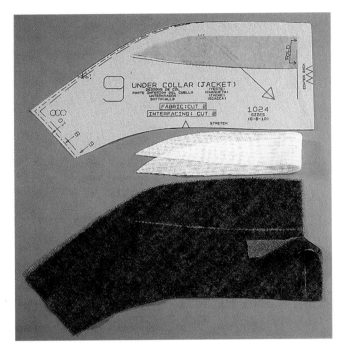

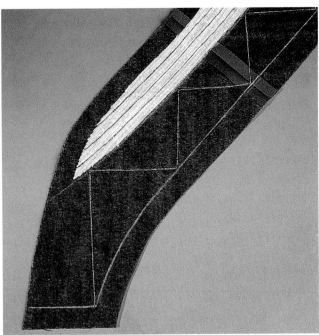

Cutting Fusible Interfacing for Collar

Cut undercollar in fusible interfacing on the bias with a center back seam. Mark the roll line, using tracing wheel and paper. Trim away the ⅝" (15 mm) center back seam allowance. Cut an additional piece of interfacing for the collar stand: using the undercollar pattern as a guide, cut the stand interfacing in one piece on the cross grain, eliminating seam allowance at center back by folding pattern in half.

Finishing the Fused Undercollar

Padstitch undercollar through all layers by machine after fusing. Stitch collar stand, using a length of 2.5 (12 stitches per inch), stitching lines ¼" (6 mm) apart, parallel to roll line, using width of foot as a guide, and ending at seam. Mark fall as pictured, following straight of grain, and forming triangle grid. Stitch fall along these lines from center back to seamline, ending stitching at seamline. Shape over ham as for custom tailoring.

FUSING TIPS

- Position fusible side of interfacing against wrong side of warmed fabric.
- Use temperature and moisture (misting, damp press cloth, or no moisture), as recommended by manufacturer.
- Use a press cloth between iron and interfacing. Use a lifting motion, overlap iron strokes and fuse the recommended time—usually 10 seconds.
- To complete bond, press on right side an additional 10 seconds, using press cloth if needed.
- On long or large pieces, begin in the center and work out to the edges.
- Bubbling can be a sign of too hot an iron or a fabric that is not porous enough for the bond to hold. Peel away and try again, or try another interfacing.

Fusing Interfacing to Undercollar

Fuse interfacing to undercollar. Sew center back seam, trim to ⅜" (10 mm), press and pound with clapper. Position the stand piece; fuse.

Sewing with Real and Synthetic Leather

Both real leather and the new synthetic Ultraleather are costly, warrant pre-testing and require sewing and pressing techniques different from wovens and knits. But once you master these methods, the results can be stunning.

Ultraleather®

Even purists have been fooled by the "real" look and feel of Ultra-leather, which is easier to sew, press and care for than real leather. Ultraleather is a synthetic non-woven fabric made of polyester and polyurethane, with a super-fine knit backing—it is technically a knit. The backing is soft and comfortable and very easy to sew. The leather-like face is supple and pleasing to the touch. It is water repellent and makes beautiful rain-coats. The dominant nature of this fabric (and sister products Ultra-suede® and Facile®) is flat and two-dimensional. It does not ease well and has moderate drape. Needle holes will show if stitches are ripped, so pre-test your pattern fit and design and perfect your sewing details before beginning.

Ultraleather does not fray, so it is not necessary to finish seam edges. A Teflon®-coated foot or walking foot is essential for top-stitching. Ultraleather is suitable for entire garments—coats, jackets, skirts, pants. Contrast collars, bound buttonholes, pocket welts, bindings, piping and detailing are practical and beautiful in Ultra-leather because it can be washed or dry cleaned.

The hard-surfaced gabardine in this full-length coat is softened by the contrast of a leather collar.

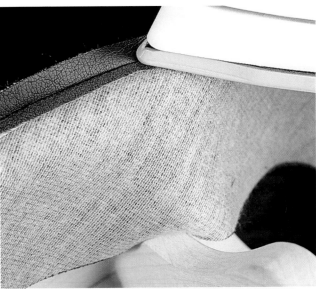

Real and synthetic leathers and suedes require special handling and sewing techniques.

Patterns and Interfacing

Neither real nor synthetic leather has a grain, so you may place pattern pieces at an off-grain angle, but use a nap layout. Leather neither frays nor eases well; stick to flat pieces and shapes.

Fusible weft interfacings (such as Suit Shaper®) work well with Ultraleather. Fuse with a press cloth and warm/wool iron setting. Use a sew-in interfacing with real leather. Attach with small dots of Sobo® glue in the seam allowances.

Sewing

Use polyester long-staple thread and stitch length 3 (10 stitches per inch) for seams. Short stitches can make perforations, causing tearing. Use a jeans needle for machine-stitching real leather; leather or "bayonet point" needles leave a larger, ragged hole more prone to tearing. With Ultraleather, use a size 12/80 universal or size 12/80 jeans needle and a standard foot when sewing on the wrong side. Use a Teflon or even-feed "walking" foot when sewing leather and when topstitching both leather and Ultraleather.

Pressing

Press real leather with a cool iron, if at all. Steam and direct contact with the iron can cause irreparable damage. Finger-press when possible. Use a Teflon sole plate on the iron and a press cloth. Keep seams flat with a

Pressing Synthetic Leather
Add fusible weft interfacing to both upper collar of Ultraleather and wool undercollar. Do not trim interfacing seam allowances. Grade seams. Press flat as sewn, then press open over point presser. Press seam allowances toward undercollar (wool). Understitch from right side using Teflon-coated foot.

light application of rubber cement and/or topstitching. Press Ultraleather with a warm iron. Test for steam and temperature. Use a press cloth on the right side. Topstitch to hold seams and edges flat.

Topstitching Synthetic Leather Collar
Press from undercollar (wool) side. Seam will roll under (or favor) about 1/8" (3 mm). Topstitch from right side using a Teflon-coated or even-feed foot and a stitch length of 4 (6 stitches per inch).

CHAPTER 7

Geoffrey Beene

With over thirty years of successful designing behind him and eight Coty Awards to his credit, Geoffrey Beene continues to display a perceptive approach to simplifying clothing for today's woman who lives in the quick-paced modern world. His are the clothes with great fashion assurance, precise detailing, supple silhouettes and a perfectionist attitude.

This chapter shows you how to duplicate the precise detailing you'd find on a Geoffrey Beene garment—dramatic bias binding and decorative tubing in contrasting fabric—as well as other professional techniques such as top-stitching and edge-stitching, plus tips on how to sew with the exciting new double-faced fabrics.

Bending the Rules with Style

The Designer at Work

A native of Louisiana, Beene had the good fortune early in his career to work for the Parisian designer Molyneux—a master of tailoring and the bias cut—before making a name for himself in New York. He began a business under his own name in 1963, and in the years since has never failed to include at least one tongue-in-cheek style to stir up otherwise elegant but always original presentations.

Beene continually questions fashion assumptions. Why do daytime clothes have to be matte and evening clothes shiny? Why is black considered boring? Why can't mohair be trimmed with lace? Why isn't comfort considered before shape? He answers these questions with collections that bend the rules but never forsake taste and quality.

Like a perceptive painter, his subtle use of the line draws attention to the right proportion and the proper look, achieving simplicity by emphasizing cut and line. He enlivens each collection with special attention to dressmaking details such as topstitching and bias bindings. He is noted for his subtle and imaginative use of color, accenting neutrals with dashes of pure intensities. For Beene the design stems from the qualities of the fabric, and he enjoys mixing "poor" and "rich" materials to achieve a contemporary look.

Beene's presentations of his designs also reflect his innovative approach to fashion. Instead of the traditional runway show of models, he presents his designs with the skill and intuition of a theatrical producer, combining performance art with mood, music, theme and color. To celebrate his thirty-year career, Beene showed a film of his three-decade collection of garments

Edgestitching and topstitching are used to enhance the clean, asymetric lines of the lapels, pockets and edge details on this suit.

in the context for which they were designed: in real life action off the runway.

Anatomy of a Beene Ensemble

In Geoffrey Beene's jacket (this page), you can see that the overlap with button closure at the neck and drawstring tie at the waist will give good protection from cold weather and gusty winds. Without looking oversized, the sleeve cut with the coat body will be comfortable over the dress. Another bonus is that you will not have to set in a sleeve! The asymmetry of the right lapel and the angle of the hemline take the eye on an interesting trip away from what could be a less-than-perfect body. This jacket could easily be shortened or lengthened. The inseam pockets are a convenience but not a tedious detail. Suggested fabric is mohair or melton. Mohair will give the jacket a softer feel and look in addition to forgiving any wayward stitches. For a less dramatic color effect, choose muted or blended colors, keeping in mind that you need to enhance your own natural coloration. This jacket could take a dramatic turn with jeans and pants as well as with skirts and sweaters.

The underlying dress (page 80) is a true testimony to Beene's philosophy that a piece of clothing should not lock a woman into a specific situation. It is feminine, and has the softness and simplicity for an all-occasion dress. It is also open to personal interpretation. Do consider a wool jersey along with the wool crepe; look for fabrics with some Lycra® blended with the wool for additional stretch. Should you prefer to have less color contrast in the hip area, consider using self-fabric for the binding and tubing for the trim and ties. When choosing your jacket and dress fabrics, play with the textures and colors until you get just the right ones for a dramatic contrast or for more of a tone-on-tone combination.

Geoffrey Beene shows his keen eye for proportion and color in this dramatic jacket and dress ensemble. It has clean lines that do not conflict with a soft femininity and it exemplifies Beene's suggestion that you take a pattern and create your own personal style through your individual changes.

Bias Binding and Tubing

Using fabric for trims such as binding or tubing is a hallmark of fine couturier clothing. A flawless execution is essential to the success of the finished look—here's how to perfect these techniques.

Bias Bindings

Bias binding provides a finish that both conceals and strengthens raw edges. Geoffrey Beene uses binding as a couture finish at a neckline or sleeve edge. He often chooses an intense color on a neutral ground for a dramatic effect.

Geoffrey Beene enlivens a subtle silhouette with a dash of color through the use of bias bindings at the neckline and sleeves, and tubing ties at the waistline.

Once you understand the method of cutting, piecing, stitching and finishing bias strips, you are ready to create endless treatments, effects and variations. Do some testing to avoid unpleasant surprises that might occur without preliminary samples.

Ease of handling and versatility make a bias binding a suitable replacement for a shaped facing. If the garment fabric is bulky or scratchy, or if it is a sheer and a wide facing would be objectionable, a bias binding of China silk or a lining fabric is an appropriate choice.

A bias binding application stabilizes an edge and can take the place of an interfacing. The flexibility of bias allows it to be shaped to go around curves that might be difficult to face. Bias can also face a hem where a turn of the fashion cloth might be too bulky.

Bias as a couture finish is often used successfully to define edges of collars, pocket flaps, edges of jackets, and pocket openings. Often these applications are of a contrasting color, a stripe, or a print fabric. As such, they are highly visible and it becomes necessary to execute all the necessary steps to insure uniformity of width in cutting, stitching, and finishing.

One of the greater satisfactions of sewing is a bias binding that turns smoothly and evenly over an edge with nary a twist, a pull, or a ripple to mar its flat surface. To achieve a perfect binding, cut strips of fabric evenly on the true bias, join them on the grain, and press and shape them before application.

CUTTING BIAS BINDING

The ideal bias strip is cut from one piece of fabric long enough to fit the desired area. However, this is not always the most economical usage of the fabric, so piecing becomes a necessity. This can be done in one of two ways—by piecing continuous strips or by cutting individual strips and piecing them together.

For either method, take a rectangular piece of fabric cut on the straight grain. Fold it diagonally at one end

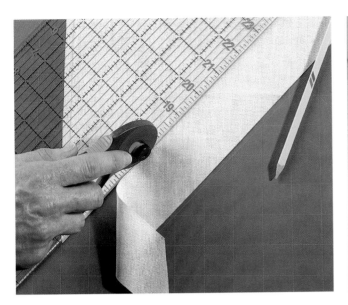

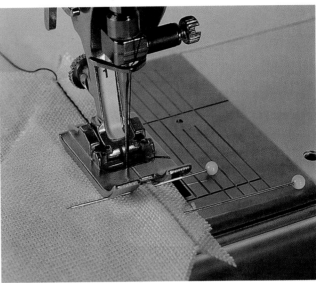

Cutting Continuous Bias Strips, Step One

Continuous pieced strips will streamline the steps to follow. Align a rectangular piece of fabric cut on the straight grain along a gridded cutting mat. Fold it diagonally at one end to determine the true bias grain. Mark the strips with a washable marking pen and cut, using a straight edge and rotary cutter.

Piecing Individual Bias Strips

Individually pieced strips are more time-consuming. Cut along the marking for the bias strips. The short ends, previously cut on the grain, will appear to be cut on the diagonal. Mark a seamline 1/4" (6 mm) from each end. With right sides of the strip together, match the seamlines (not the cut edges), pin, and stitch. Press the seam open.

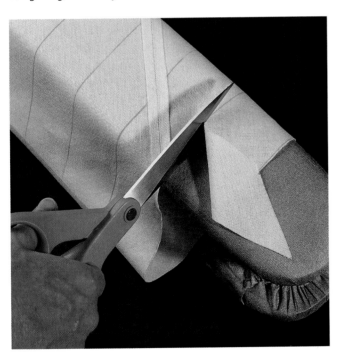

Cutting Continuous Bias Strips, Step Two

On a marked piece of fabric, join the ends to create a tube with right sides together, and one strip width extending beyond the seam at each side. Machine-stitch, using a 1/4" (6 mm) seam allowance. Press open on a sleeve board and cut with shears. Begin cutting on the marked line at one end and continue in circular fashion.

to find the true bias. Using the bias fold as a guide, mark fabric with parallel lines the desired width of the bias strips, marking as many strips as needed and allowing for 1/4" (6 mm) seams.

For traditional, *single* bias binding (the version shown in the photographs), cut the strips four times the finished width plus 1/8"–1/4" (3 mm–6 mm) extra, which is taken up as the fabric turns along the outer edge.

For *double,* or French, bias binding, cut the strips six times the finished width plus an additional 1/8"–1/4" (3 mm–6 mm).

For either style of binding, make a diagonal fold along last line of marking and cut along both folds, discarding the triangular ends. Mark a 1/4" (6 mm) seamline on both ends.

PRESSING BIAS BINDING

To prepare the traditional single binding, fold the outside edges of the newly cut bias to the center, leaving a space for the middle fold. Press. A bias tape maker (in 1/2"/13 mm, 1"/25 mm, and 2"/5 cm widths) insures uniformity of folded binding. Press strip in half again lengthwise, with one edge slightly wider than the other.

To prepare double (French) binding, fold the cut strip in half lengthwise first; and then in thirds.

APPLYING BIAS BINDING

When applying bias binding to a neckline or hem edge, it is important to remember to trim the garment seam allowance away before attaching the bias finish.

On curves, it's a good idea to pre-shape the bias with light steam. Shape the folded center edge of the bias to match the cut edge of the garment. As you pre-shape the bias, do not stretch it much; you risk shrinking it in width. When pre-shaping, your objective is to create a corresponding shape which matches the curve of the garment edge.

Pre-shaping the Binding
With the pattern pieces pinned together, mark the seamline on the pattern. This will become the finished edge. Shape the binding to conform to the finished edge (neckline) using steam, without placing the weight of the iron on the cloth.

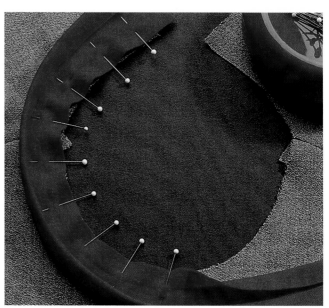

Pinning Binding to Garment
With right sides together, open binding and match raw edge to the neck edge. Pin from the binding side with pins perpendicular to the edge. Allow ¹/₂" (13 mm) seam allowance at the ends of the binding to turn inside.

Sewing Binding to Garment
Baste the binding to the garment edge without stretching. Machine-stitch exactly along the fold.

Overlapping Binding at Hem
On hems, join the binding by folding under one side on the straight grain and lapping the other side over, then machine-stitching them together on the fold. Trim to ¹/₄" (6 mm); press open.

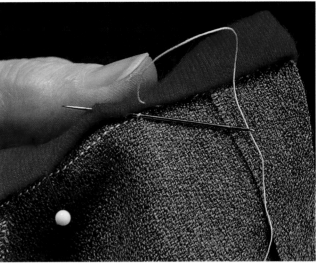

Turning Binding Inside

With the tip of the iron, meld the stitches. Using a tailor's ham will help you avoid placing the iron flat on the cloth. Turn short ends of the binding to inside so the binding edge is even with the garment edge. Press. Grade excess only at the ends. Turn binding to the inside. Pin.

Slipstitching Binding to Garment

To slipstitch, insert the needle under one machine stitch, then through the binding fold every $1/4$" (6 mm). Do not pull thread tight; it should be invisible on both sides. Use small stitches at the ends.

FINISHING BIAS BINDING

For single binding, you will need to decide whether to finish the edge of binding by hand or machine. Hand sewing is finer and less conspicuous, but the stitch-in-the-ditch option offers durability and saves time. For double binding, finish the remaining long edge of binding by hand.

SYNTHETIC LEATHER BINDING

You can use synthetic suedes or leathers such as Ultrasuede® for a bound edge finish. The advantage of these "fabrics" is that they do not ravel, have less bulk, and application is simpler. The binding requires only a single fold with no seam allowances.

To create a $1/2$" (13 mm) wide finished binding, cut the binding strip $1 1/2$" (3.8 cm) wide. (That's $1/2$"/13 mm plus extra $1/8$"/3 mm for front, and $1/2$"/13 mm plus extra $3/8$"/10 mm for the back.) Cut the strip on the crosswise grain; piece strips by lapping $1/4$" (6 mm) on the diagonal.

After trimming the seam allowances off the garment edges to be bound, fold the binding strips lengthwise with wrong sides together, with $5/8$" (15 mm) on one side (the top side) and $7/8$" (22 mm) on the other (the back). Baste binding to garment edge. Edgestitch, using a Teflon® or walking foot, a size 70/11 needle and polyester thread. On wrong side, trim off $1/4$" (6 mm) along inside edge of binding, using appliqué scissors.

You may wish to use a wider binding on heavy, bulky fabrics. Note: This binding is not suitable for sharp curves.

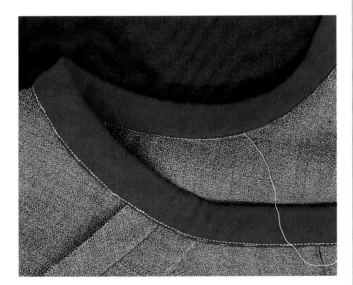

Stitch-in-the-Ditch Option

If you choose this option, you must press the bias so that it is $1/8$" (3 mm) wider on one side (the inside). Baste and attach binding to garment as with previous application. Machine-stitch from the outside in the seam to catch the binding on the inside. Slipstitch the ends.

Decorative Tubing

Decorative tubing formed with bias strips adds an impressive touch to a simple style. It can be self-filled or filled with cord, and made in contrasting or self-fabric. You may also use purchased braid or other tubular material that complements your garment fabric for the same effect.

CORD-FILLED TUBING

To make heavier corded tubing, cut a bias strip of fabric the desired length, wide enough to fit around the cord plus $^1/_2$" (13 mm) for seam allowances. Cut a piece of cable cord twice the length of the bias; the extra cord will facilitate stitching and turning. Fold the bias over the cord with the right sides together and the edges even. Using a zipper foot, stitch across the end through the cording. Pivot, then stretch the bias slightly while stitching the long edge close to the cording. Trim the seam allowance. To turn right side out, slowly draw the enclosed cord out of the tubing; the free cord will be pulled into the tubing automatically. Cut off the stitched end and the excess cording.

SELF-FILLED TUBING

Cut a bias strip the desired length and the finished width plus enough seam allowance to fill the tubing. The amount of seam allowance depends upon your fabric—the bulkier the fabric, the narrower the seam allowances. Experiment to determine the correct width for your particular fabric. Remember also that the strip will become slightly narrower as it stretches in length during stitching.

An easy way to construct a self-filled tube is to knot the end of a long cordonnet thread and securely stitch it to the end of the bias strip. With right sides together, fold bias in half lengthwise. Place the cordonnet along the inside, next to the fold. At the end, slant the stitching diagonally to catch the cordonnet and close off the end. Stitch long edges of bias together. Trim bulk from the end with the attached cord. To turn, pull the cordonnet and ease the tubing through itself. Cut off the cord end, turn in $^1/_4$" (6 mm) of end and slipstitch closed.

Turning Tube Inside Out
Trim seam to a scant $^1/_4$" (6 mm). Trim bulk from the end with the attached cord. Pull end of cord to turn seam inside. Cut off cord end. Turn in $^1/_4$" (6 mm) at ends of tube and slipstitch.

Securing Cord to Fabric
With the end of cordonnet securely fastened to one short end of the fabric, stitch long edges together. (Do not catch cord in the stitching.) Leave remaining end open.

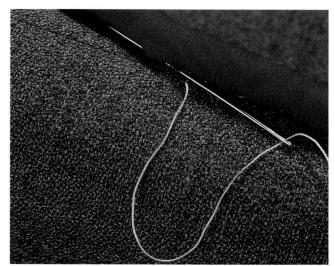

Attaching Tubing to Garment
On outside of garment, slipstitch trim in place.

Finishing Touches

Often a neckline edge or waistband requires a hook and eye fastener. To be truly functional, it should be chosen in a size appropriate for the fabric weight and the amount of strain the closure will receive. The closure should be inconspicuous and the hand stitches that hold the hook in place should never penetrate to the outside of the garment. Before you begin sewing with a *matching thread* and a strong knot, run the entire length of thread over beeswax. This not only makes the thread easier to pull through the eyes, but it prevents agonizing tangles and knots. Hide the knots and ends by running them between the layers of fabric and clipping them off close to the surface.

Sew the hook in place first and then determine whether you will want a metal eye or a thread eye which will be more flexible and less conspicuous. The advantage of the thread eye is that you can place it at the edges of an opening that just meet (as opposed to edges that lap). With the hook in its proper place (slightly back from the edge) and the loop extending slightly beyond the edge, the opening edges will be side by side without a gap.

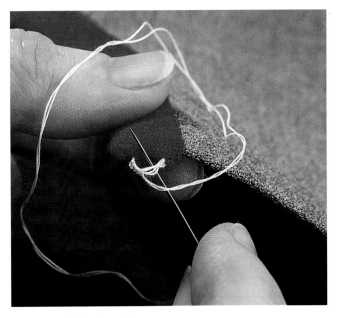

Blanket-stitch Thread Eye
Make a blanket-stitch loop by taking two or three foundation stitches the desired length and depth of the loop; secure the ends with small backstitches. Then work blanket stitches the length of the foundation thread. Run needle to the inside to conceal the thread ends.

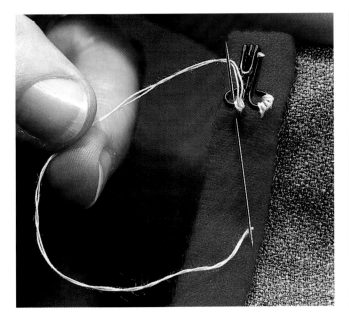

Attaching a Hook
To attach the hook, use waxed thread and work stitches around the circular holes, taking care not sew through to the outside of the garment. Take several stitches to hold the hook end flat.

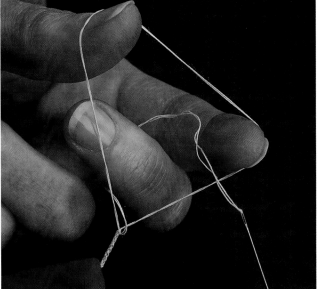

Crochet-stitch Thread Eye
Create a thread chain by securing the ends, then forming a loop on the right side of fabric by taking another short stitch. Slip your thumb and first two fingers of your left hand through the loop while holding the needle and thread in your right hand. Using the second finger of your left hand, pick up a new loop and pull it through the first loop, tightening as you proceed. Continue to work the chain to the desired length. Place the needle through the first loop to form a knot. Secure with several small stitches.

Topstitching and Edgestitching

The most popular form of fashion stitchery, topstitching emphasizes the structural lines of your garment while working to keep the seams and edges flat and crisp. Although done by machine, it gives the same detailed look as fine hand sewing.

Both topstitching and edgestitching can be done after the garment is completed, but it is often necessary or easier to stitch individual or large areas during construction. Make any fitting adjustments before you topstitch seams. Don't forget that it is often a construction procedure in such features as pockets, pleats and man-tailored shirts.

Use silk buttonhole twist, a size 16 needle and a stitch length of 3.5–4 (6–8 stitches per inch). You will probably have to loosen your machine tension. Before stitching, experiment first on scrap layers of your fabric and underlining. Stitch carefully, using a guide such as a quilting foot, magnet, tape, etc. Be particularly cautious at curves and pivot the fabric at corners; mark these tricky areas with silk thread tracing before stitching. Stitch two lines very close together on heavy-weight fabrics. Leave thread ends long enough to be pulled to the wrong side with a needle and tied.

The prominence of edgestitching requires that the seam be properly prepared. After machine-stitching, press the seam as stitched to meld the stitches, then press the seam open over a point presser before turning the facing to the inside. An edgestitch foot is designed to help you sew straight lines along the edge. (You may find it easier to baste with silk thread to hold the shape while edgestitching.)

Edgestitching
The edgestitching foot assures that the stitching will be parallel to the edge. In general, use matching sewing thread for edgestitching.

Topstitching
Topstitching may require heavier thread to make it stand out. Buttonhole twist usually works well in matching or contrasting colors. Use cotton thread in the bobbin. Increase the stitch length for topstitching. Bury thread ends by pulling them to the inside with a needle. You may find it helpful to mark topstitching lines with silk basting thread (to be removed after machine-stitching).

PROFESSIONAL PRESSING TIPS

To avoid costly mistakes, use your scraps to test the limits of the fabric. A see-through press cloth will prevent a hard shine; a damp press cloth will direct moisture to specific areas where you want it. Avoid heavy concentrations of steam on wool crepes and silks, which will readily shrink.

Strictly defined, pressing means raising and lowering the iron, not pushing it, which tends to create ripples and distortion.

After stitching, immediately press the seam allowance and the stitching line with the point of the iron in the direction it was stitched, on both sides, to meld or flatten it. Press enclosed seams open before turning or pressing them closed. This should be done on a surface shaped like the seam—a point presser, ham, seam roll, etc. Press before trimming; then grade, clip, and re-press if necessary.

Always let your garment cool and dry before moving it. A wooden clapper will help here; it absorbs moisture while further flattening the crease or a detail.

Double Cloth

Double cloth is exciting because—generally—it is reversible and eliminates the need for interfacings, facings and lining. A few new construction pointers are essential.

Fabric and Styles

Double cloth usually appears in coating weights, but occasionally you may find it in a suit weight. The fabric consists of two layers of fabric either fused together or joined by an extra set of yarns during weaving. The layers may be the same fabric on both sides, or two dramatically different fabrics such as a plaid and a plain fabric.

Because double cloth does not drape well, choose garment styles that are simple, with few details. Patch pockets, shawl collars, raglan and kimono sleeves, and wrap styles are good choices. Patterns appropriate for crisp fabrics will usually work.

Construction

To begin construction of edges and seams, separate the two layers about $1^{1}/_{2}$" (3.8 cm) by pulling the layers apart. For cloth that has been joined by extra yarns, clip these yarns with small scissors. Decide which side of the fabric will be the "right" or outer layer for construction purposes.

For a *plain, flat seam,* stitch the right sides of the outer layer, using a $^{5}/_{8}$" (15 mm) seam allowance. Trim $^{1}/_{4}$" (6 mm) off both sides of the remaining layer, turn the edges under, and slipstitch the folded edges together. Other appropriate seams include flat-felled, lapped, strapped, or decoratively serged or topstitched.

Along curved seams, staystitch the two pieces of fabric after separating the layers, clipping as necessary.

Finish edges by turning the two layers to the inside along the seamline or hem, and slipstitch. Eliminate bulk by trimming one edge $^{1}/_{4}$" (6 mm) before turning. You may also insert piping between the two layers before slipstitching, or you may bind the edge with the same or contrasting fabric, including real and synthetic suedes and leathers, and purchased braids and trims.

To *insert a finished piece* such as a collar, match seamlines. Machine-stitch one set of layers together, turn one side of remaining layers under and slipstitch or edgestitch to the other side close to the fold.

Separating the Layers
Separate the layers for $1^{1}/_{2}$" (6 mm) and clip the extra yarns that weave the layers together.

Making Seams
Stitch one layer, using a $^{5}/_{8}$" (15 mm) seam allowance; press open. Trim the remaining layer $^{1}/_{4}$" (6 mm), turning the edges over the first seam and slipstitching.

Finishing Edges
Turn the two layers inside along the seamline or hem; slipstitch the folded edges together.

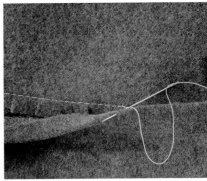

Inserting a Collar
Staystitch the two layers and clip as necessary. Machine-stitch one set of layers together, matching seamlines. Turn remaining layer under and slipstitch or edgestitch.

CHAPTER 8

Todd Oldham

To someone who loves to sew, studying Todd Oldham and learning about what inspires him is a delight. He is full of surprises in his offbeat sensibility of finding charm and interest in the mundane. The inventive wit and originality that he presents to women's fashion design continually earns him praise from the critics.

Oldham's sense of style translates perfectly into the language of the home sewer who likes to combine many personal elements into a fashion statement. In this chapter, you'll learn how to piece your own one-of-a-kind fabric, experiment with novelty button and closure treatments, and master the art of sewing sheer fabrics flawlessly.

Fashion Fun with Details

The Designer at Work

Todd Oldham's grandmother taught him to sew at a young age, and he was soon designing dresses from Op Art pillow cases for his sister. After a brief stay in the Alterations Department at The Ralph Lauren Polo Shop in Dallas, in 1981 Oldham borrowed $100 from his parents and purchased 40 yards of cotton knit fabric, hand-dyed it in his bathtub and made some split skirts and T-shirts to launch his first collection, purchased by Neiman Marcus. By 1988, he was established in New York, and founded Times 7, which began as a women's shirt collection.

The fashion silhouettes he designs are simple, classic and uncomplicated, but he has fun with fabric and details. One of his signature pieces is a great white shirt, but an inventive touch is added with novelty buttons. Oldham's buttons, available to the home sewer, include motifs of dogs and dog bones (with jewels, of course), timepieces, teapots, fruits and vegetables, handbags and shoes. The more humorous the better! Oldham's inspirations for his buttons and clothes come from thrift stores, vintage home furnishings, people on the street and his penchant for arts and crafts.

He loves to mix things up and allow everyone to look like they came from the other side of time. He may cut up an old style to create something new, like taking the chiffon sleeves of an old dress and adding them to the body of a tailored jacket, or cutting up an old shirt and adding it to a favorite skirt to make a new dress. He's even been known to make clothes out of cork, pot holders, and Persian rugs. Each season's collection is created around a theme, such as "Interiors" or "Garage Sale."

The future is bright for this young designer. He has already received the Perry Ellis Award for New Fashion Talent from the Council of Fashion Designers of America and been named Rising Star by the Dallas Fashion Awards.

Todd Oldham's innovative use of exotic fabrics is shown in the flowing, semi-sheer, wide pants combined with a rich Thai silk vest that features his novelty buttons.

Oldham's New Approaches

Todd Oldham's unconventional approach breaks traditional rules of sewing, color and fabric combinations. He feels that there are no rules anymore. To duplicate his work, you may want to try using vegetables such as beets as an unorthodox dye for ordinary fabric. Look through remnant piles in thrift shops and start mixing and color-blocking fabrics. Use old fabrics from your "stash" or cut from vintage clothing that you may not wish to use as a total garment, but might be the perfect addition to a group of textures and colors. This is an opportunity to personalize your fabrics. Oldham says, "Home sewing is the closest to couture that you can get."

One of Oldham's favorite ways to invent a look is to mix subtle tonal patterns. Damasks and jacquard weaves are good examples of tone-on-tone fabrics. Choose two or more fabrics in the same color value, but change the scale of the print, mixing large with small. A jacket might be made in a larger scale version of the same small-scale print used in the skirt. Or reverse the fabric if it is woven, using one side of the fabric for one garment piece and the other side of the fabric for the second coordinating garment.

Observing his approach to mixing fabrics and colors inspires you to loosen up and begin reaching across the ordinary boundaries of fabric combinations. Use pieces of tapestry and brocade to create your own patchwork fabric for a unique vest. Combine that with a crushed velvet tiered skirt or pants and that great white shirt with the interesting buttons. Look to interior design for avant-garde fabric combinations such as wide stripe silks for pants, renaissance motifs on lightweight damasks for vests and jackets, and bold colors and patterns in sheers and silks. Even Oldham's jacket linings and vest backs sport other designs and colors—a leopard print is a favorite. Oldham has a sense of humor and *joie de vivre* in his designs, and so can you. This designer encourages you to break the rules, experiment, take chances, make some mistakes and use those mistakes to create a detail—they can be charming.

Todd Oldham's signature white shirt is embellished with a collection of his unique buttons featuring fruits and vegetables.

DESIGNER SEWING TECHNIQUES

Designing Pieced Fabric

Although creating a new fabric from remnants at hand has come a long way from our great-grandmothers' quilts, it still remains a satisfying way of playing with color, motifs and texture, and is right at home in contemporary fashion.

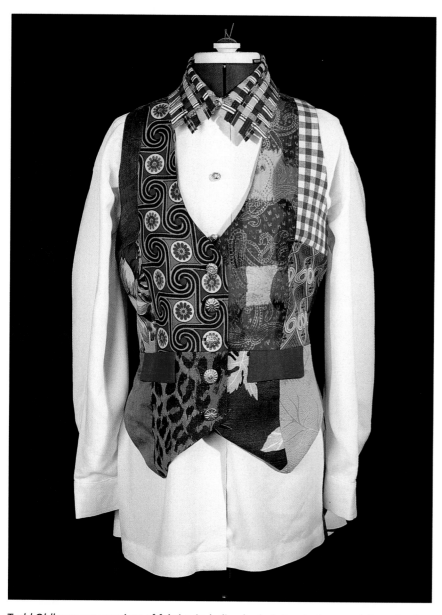

Todd Oldham uses a variety of fabrics, including bark cloth, gingham and damask. His unusual combinations of colors and motifs illustrate his innovative approach to design in this Times 7 vest.

Selecting fabrics, deciding on a color scheme and planning a design for a "new fabric" is very much like decorating a room or painting a picture. It's an art. You must draw upon basic design principles or rely on your own inherent design instincts. People who are instinctively creative often do not know how they arrive at various choices. Those who consider themselves devoid of creativity do not know how to start making creative choices. But you can learn designing if you adhere to a few fundamental design theories.

A Todd Oldham design—as illustrated by his choice of fabrics and colors in the Times 7 vest pictured here—may look as if he designs instinctively and without regard for design principles. He has chosen fabrics that at first glance are very different and unrelated. But upon closer study, you realize that the total effect works, and that, in fact, basic principles may be identified in the relationship of the various fabric selections.

Notice that the shapes of the pieces are symmetrical from one side of the vest to the other. The left side of the vest has the same number, size and shape of pieces as the right side. There is *order in the shapes* despite the fabric mixture.

All the fabrics—primarily silk and cotton—have the *same weight*. All the pieces feel similar; certain ones do not stand out as lacking in substance or being too bulky—there is a visual sameness in weight. If you like a fabric that is more lightweight than the others in your selection, you can back it with fusible interfacing or backing fabrics such as batiste or muslin in order to make it approximately the same weight as the others.

Observe the matter of *scale* in Oldham's motif selection. He selects a primary design of medium scale, then chooses other designs that mirror it. In this case, the primary design is a concentric circle/swirl motif that is repeated in a different color and size in a second fabric. The curved outlines in these two fabrics show up again as organic motifs of leaves and animal skins in other fabrics, both in the print and tone-on-tone fabrics. Two abstract, watery designs help soften and blend the hard edges of the pattern pieces. The surprise element—a red and white gingham—actually helps hold the *symmetry* in the overall relationship of the pieces. If the scale of some of the prints is small, then the color is strong, or there is real contrast to *balance* the larger scale of the primary design.

The powerful colors—primarily red and green—are lively and vibrant because they are contrasting colors on opposite sides of the color wheel. The deep red damask piece that has such strength bal-

ances with the red and white gingham at the opposite corner. The neutrals soothe and cool the effect of the other fabrics, but they hold their own because of their scale or the saturation of their color.

Oldham's Signature Fabrics, Colors and Combos
Not only does Oldham mix fabrics and patterns in an ensemble, but he creates his own fabric by cutting strips of fabric and sewing them together in blocks, then cuts the garment out of the "new" fabric. Notice that he deliberately uses the wrong side of some fabrics, and mixes the lengthwise and crosswise grains.

A VEST WITH A SPECIAL TOUCH

Why not change the traditional way of belting the back of a vest? In a recent collection of vests, Oldham has inserted fabric loops into dart seams or princess-line seams through which fabric cording is laced and tied. Consider alternatives to the self-fabric tie by using rattail trims, braided rayon seam binding or interesting vintage cordings and laces.

Creative Touches

Buttons and their closures make their own statement—dramatic, funny or beautiful—on an otherwise simple garment. Here are some ideas to spur your creativity and inspire a unique treatment.

Buttons

Todd Oldham introduced his signature "great white shirt" with the debut of Times 7, his sportswear line. In typical Oldham style, the classic and understated shirt was simply a canvas for his entertaining buttons. Oldham's buttons are made especially for his collection and Times 7 lines. Early on, he made buttons out of glass, twigs, and cast white metals. Recycling is an important issue with him, so he encourages people to make buttons out of bottle caps, rocks, or other found objects. And he advises you to save those great buttons from old clothing to reuse again.

Go ahead and change the number of buttons on a garment. The front of a shirt may have twelve buttons—five that actually button and the remaining buttons sewn on for novelty. Cuffs look great with more than one button. Cluster small buttons in groups of three. Make your own button covers so that you can change the mood of a garment when you wish. Sew ordinary shirt buttons in rows at the edge of a collar or cuff of a jacket to create a line of trim. Oldham states, "What I love about my buttons is that they make perfect decoys if you make a mistake. They're great at covering up the bruises."

An Oldham Collection
The Todd Oldham Collection of buttons is whimsical, old worldly, witty and definitely original. Use them as a set, or mix sizes, shapes, and themes.

A Vintage Collection
Oldham's designs reflect his love for arts and crafts and vintage treasures. Coins and quirky charms were some of the first buttons Oldham used in his Times 7 line of shirts.

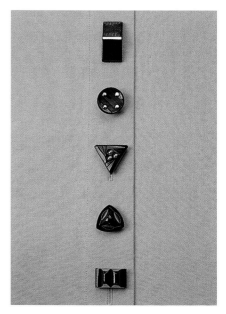

A Personal Collection
Personalize your own great shirt with interesting buttons collected from the attic or flea markets.

Closures

A buttonhole can be anything but ordinary and purely functional. Creative closures are an interesting way to add detail to spare shapes.

When edging a garment with cording, leave unsewn spaces that can be used as a button opening. Conceal buttonholes within a vertical or horizontal seam by simply leaving a slotted opening.

LOOP BUTTONHOLES

Make loop buttonholes out of self fabric, purchased trims, ribbons, braids and cords. When using self fabric, select the appropriate size of cotton cable cord or rattail filler in keeping with the scale of the fabric. A bulky fabric requires a larger diameter filler.

CONTRASTING NOVELTY BUTTONHOLES

Bound buttonholes do not have to match the fashion fabric. Choose contrasting fabrics in solid colors or prints, leather and synthetic suedes, or striped and plaid fabrics cut on the straight of grain or bias. Change the scale by altering the width of the lips from the norm and you have a dynamic detail. Triangles, trapezoids, circles and half-circles are optional bound buttonhole shapes.

FROG CLOSURES

Frog closures are historical garment details that can be modernized in a clever way. One possibility: secure a brass toggle from the hardware store with strips of synthetic suede through slits or buttonholes in the fabric.

Loop Buttonhole
Set fabric loops in the facing seam on one side of the garment, allowing for the scale of your button.

Contrasting Bound Buttonholes
Use a different fabric for bound buttonholes. Here is a striped fabric used both on-grain and on the bias.

A Modern Frog Closure
Oldham buttons are used in a decorative way as trim to give this ordinary piece a glamorous touch.

TIPS FOR PERFECTLY PLACED BUTTONS

Place the top buttonhole at least half the width of the button plus 1/4" (6 mm) from the top edge. Place the last buttonhole 3"–4" (7.5 cm–10 cm) from the bottom edge, never through the hem; omit the last buttonhole if necessary. Place buttons no closer than 5/8" (15 mm) from the closing edge. For a large button, the extension from the end of the buttonhole to the closing edge should be a minimum of half the button's width plus 1/4" (6 mm).

MEASURING SPECIALTY BUTTONS

Buttons such as those featured in Todd Oldham's collection may be irregular in size and require special measuring. Make a few test samples. Wrap a narrow strip of paper around the button at its largest diameter or widest width. Where the two sides meet, mark with pins or marking pen. Open out paper, then fold in half, matching marks. Measure from fold to mark (half the diameter). Add 1/8" (3 mm) to determine correct buttonhole size.

Topstitching

Topstitching on thick fabrics can present problems: either the presser foot does not want to move the fabric along to create an even stitch, or the stitches get buried and do not show. Sometimes the thread frays or breaks. There are several presser feet that aid considerably in eliminating these problems. The walking foot or even-feed foot feeds the top and bottom layers of fabric evenly and moves the fabric along more easily. The roller foot and the Teflon®-coated foot also keep the layers from shifting and lessen the "drag" against the underside of a conventional presser foot.

Updated vintage details and interesting fabric create an avant-garde styling. Note the two sets of novelty buttons.

An often-overlooked foot is the straight-stitch foot. Using the narrow right side of the foot as a guide, you can avoid sliding off the inner trimmed seam of a facing or turned edge.

There are special topstitching needles for heavy fabrics. Choose among sizes 90/14, 100/16, 110/18 and 130/N. A topstitching needle has a long eye and a deeper scarf or groove that allows a heavier thread to pass through it easily, eliminating fraying and broken threads.

You will need to experiment with different thread options to achieve the look that you want. Traditional cordonnet thread is a 30-weight and three-ply (30/3) polyester thread, available in many colors to coordinate or contrast with your fabric. Buttonhole silk is an eight-weight, three-ply thread that provides an especially lustrous finish, and is also available in many colors. Metallic thread wrapped with cotton or other fiber can be used with a special size 80 needle designed for metallics. This needle is Teflon-coated, with a longer, deeper scarf and very long eye.

A UNIQUE TOPSTITCHING TREATMENT

Couched Zigzag with Embroidery Foot
For a decorative approach, use an embroidery foot with a small hole in the body of the foot, and feed cordonnet thread through the hole in the foot, then "couch" over it with a fine zigzag stitch. Trim one seam allowance to ¼" (6 mm) and leave the other seam allowance untrimmed. This will eliminate the tendency of the presser foot to fall away from the edge as you topstitch.

Sewing with Sheers

As sheer fabrics such as chiffon and georgette gain popularity in the ready-to-wear industry, you'll need to know how to handle these special fabrics.

Seams for Sheers

Because of the transparency of sheers, seams need to be delicate and finely finished. The traditional French seam is commonly used in couture clothing and is perfect for the heavier double chiffons and georgettes. There are two techniques for constructing a French seam.

TRADITIONAL FRENCH SEAM

The traditional method involves sewing a $3/8"$ (10 mm) seam with the wrong sides together. Trim the seam to $1/8"$ (2 mm) and press flat. Separate the two pieces of the garment and press the seam in the direction it needs to lie for the next step in construction.

Press the right sides together and stitch along the seamline

Traditional French Seam, Step 1
Trim the first seam close to stitching, about $1/4"$ (3 mm).

$1/8"$–$1/4"$ (3 mm–6 mm) from first stitching, encasing the trimmed seam. An edgestitch foot with the needle position all the way to the left aids in the stitching process. Again, press the seam in the direction it needs to lie.

Traditional French Seam, Step 2
Stitch the second seam, completely encasing the first seam and seam allowance.

SERGED FRENCH SEAM

A variation of the same French seam technique is to serge a $3/8"$ seam using a two- or three-thread rolled hem stitch on your serger. Narrow the cutting width by adjusting the cutting knife, and shorten the stitch length. Continue the process as described for the traditional French seam. The final seam encases the rolled edge. This method eliminates the need to trim the first seam and you can achieve a much narrower seam with no "hairs" poking through the second seam.

Serged French Seam
Follow the same steps as for the traditional French seam. The serger will do the trimming for you in the first step.

ZIGZAGGED SEAM

This seam option is even finer than a French seam, and should be used for the most delicate and transparent sheers. It involves stitching two rows with a standard machine. Sew a $5/8"$ (15 mm) seam with a very narrow zigzag stitch. Next to the small zigzag, sew another slightly wider zigzag. Trim close to the second zigzag and press.

Zigzagged Seam
Trim very close to the second line of zigzag stitches.

Hems for Sheers

Hems in sheer fabrics may look daunting, but the following methods produce beautiful results with minimum effort. Before hemming skirts and pants in sheer fabrics, it is always a good idea to let the garment hang for a day or two. You will need help in marking the hem; a pin-type skirt marker is a useful piece of equipment for this.

ZIGZAG HEM, METHOD ONE

For a simple but fine zigzag hem, position the needle off center to the left. Fold the fabric along the marked hemline, set the sewing machine to a very narrow zigzag stitch, and edgestitch. The blade on the edgestitch foot allows you to sew evenly along the fold of the fabric. When stitching, the needle should be off the fabric on the right-hand side of the fold. The stitch quality and fluidity of the edge is improved by using two-ply mercerized cotton embroidery thread.

On the inside, trim the excess fabric close to the zigzag stitching, using appliqué scissors. These scissors eliminate cutting into the outer fabric.

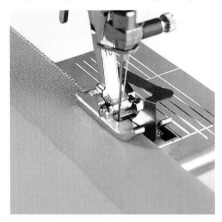

Zigzag Hem, Method One, Step One
Stitch a narrow zigzag along fold of fabric.

Zigzag Hem, Method One, Step Two
Trim close to zigzag stitching, using appliqué scissors.

ZIGZAG HEM, METHOD TWO

An alternate zigzag hem finish has a little weight to it and finishes with no raw edges. Stitch through a single layer of fabric along the marked, finished length line. This creates a staystitching line which stabilizes the fabric for the next steps. (Do not eliminate this step.)

Fold the fabric to the inside, using the staystitching line as a guide. Stitch with an edgestitch foot and needle position to the left, next to the fold. With appliqué scissors, trim close to the stitching.

Fold again, turning no more than 1/8" (3 mm), and stitch along the folded edge. You will see one row of stitching on the outside of the garment and two rows of stitching on the inside of the hem.

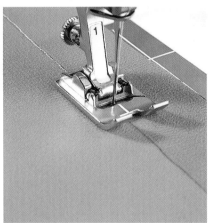

Zigzag Hem, Method Two, Step One
Staystitch along desired hemline.

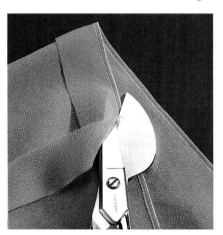

Zigzag Hem, Method Two, Step Two
After folding and stitching, trim close to second stitching.

Zigzag Hem, Method Two, Step Three
Fold once again and stitch along previous stitching.

TRIPLE NEEDLE HEM

The same process can have a slightly different look by using a 130/ 705 H/DRI 2.5/80 triple lingerie needle, which has three needles on a single shank; add the third thread source by winding an extra bobbin and putting it under one of the two thread spools. Two-ply cotton mercerized embroidery thread is also appropriate for this technique. Stitch along the folded edge and trim the remaining hem allowance on the underside next to the stitching, again using appliqué scissors.

If your machine has a double needle feature, try using it for a narrower and finer width of buttonhole. The newest computerized sewing machines have a delicate buttonhole style already programmed. Trim the transparent stabilizer and the organza close to the machine stitches.

It is always a good idea to practice the buttonholes on a scrap of fabric first. Trying to remove a botched buttonhole from a sheer fabric is impossible.

Triple Needle Hem
Trim close to straight stitching, using appliqué scissors.

Buttonhole on Sheer Fabric
Stitch buttonholes over a strip of Solvy, using organza as an interfacing.

Buttonholes on Sheers

Buttonholes in sheer fabrics require special attention. Select the machine setting for lightweight buttonholes, and limit them in size to not longer than $5/8"$ (15 mm). In sheers, buttonholes work best when horizontal so that the button will rest on a stabilized stitch line.

Insert one or two layers of organza between the two layers of fabric, depending on the weight of your sheer. Place a strip of transparent stabilizer such as Solvy® on the right side of the garment and mark the buttonhole placement with a disappearing-ink pen. Before stitching your buttonhole, it is a good idea to baste all of the layers together, including the transparent stabilizer.

NEEDLES AND THREADS FOR SHEERS

A fine needle such as a 50/6, 60/8, 65/9, or 70/10 is necessary. (The lower the number, the finer the needle.) You may use a regular cotton or polyester thread, but also try a two-ply, fine-weight silk, rayon or cotton embroidery thread. A regular stitch length should work, but you can always experiment. If your sewing machine comes with an optional throat plate with a single hole, now is the time to use it so that the fabric will not be pulled into a too-wide needle hole.

CHAPTER 9

Bill Blass

Designer Bill Blass has helped define American dressing, emphasizing the simplicity of clean lines, and allowing gorgeous fabric and great fit to characterize his fashion statement. His garments are at once strictly modern yet enduring in a timeless sense.

Clean lines require simple details, flawlessly executed. The patch pocket has long been a favorite detail for Blass and the women who wear his creations. No fewer than four methods are presented in this chapter to show you how to sew perfectly shaped pockets to accent a jacket. You'll also learn how to line a dress with ease.

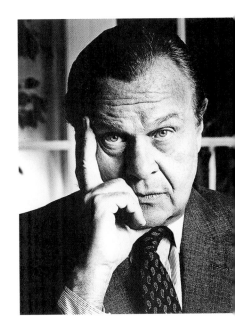

The Modern Minimalist

This contemporary suit reflects the Blass attitude toward overall simplicity, but shows his attention to detail. The curved pockets are focal points and the curved hems echo the curved theme. Both require careful sewing skills.

The Designer at Work

Regarded as the quintessential American designer, Bill Blass has sustained a simple recognizable elegance for over forty years in the fashion trade. Despite his considerable talent, Blass is almost deprecating about his contribution; he calls his body of work a craft, not an art form. In his estimation, only a few designers such as Grés or Balenciaga deserve to be called artists.

Perhaps his unassuming manner is rooted in his origins in the American Midwest. As a child in Fort Wayne, Indiana, Blass attended movies on Saturday afternoons, soaking up the fantastic elegance of the beautifully attired movie stars of the day. His childhood sketches reflected the impact of this cosmopolitan glamour. By age 15 he was selling sketches for $25 to Seventh Avenue designers. Upon graduation he boarded a train for New York City, attended school for a short time there and worked as a sketcher and designer.

After a stint in the Army during World War II, Blass returned to Seventh Avenue and worked at several design firms, increasing his skills as well as his visibility. In a time when designers were often kept anonymous by the manufacturers who employed them, the recognizable Blass style began to change the face of American fashion. His clothes were simple and elegant in line. He worked with clear colors and favored natural materials such as wool, silk, linen and cotton.

In 1959, when Blass was the head designer of Anna Miller, Ltd., the owner resigned and the company merged with Maurice Rentner. Blass remained; his name appeared on the label, and his identity emerged through clever ads with copy such as "Positively Blassfamous." Eventually, in 1970, Blass purchased the company, renaming it Bill Blass, Ltd. Today it occupies four floors of a building on Seventh Avenue.

Blass is the sole owner and president of a multi-million dollar conglomerate, which oversees about three dozen licensees nationally and 70 world-wide licensees garnering approximately $200 million annually. The licenses range from sheets to chocolates to cars and provide Blass with an annual income of more than $3 million.

Sketching continues to be his laboratory for ideas. He finds inspiration in the world around him, and is especially inspired by museums. As he told *W,* "...I have sketch pads here and there and I'm always drawing. I sketch while I'm talking on the telephone, while I'm in a car, while I'm on a plane. I sketch dresses, shoes, hats, anything and everything that might be appealing as a silhouette." The sketches are quite small, and after deciding which will work in a collection, Blass enlarges the sketch, attaches a fabric he has selected,

then turns it over to an assistant. "...I don't oversee them as they're being worked on. They're not interesting to me at that stage. They're like children when they're toddling. They're not interesting until they get up and walk. I leave them alone until the first fitting."

The Blass Fashion Philosophy

In an interview Bill Blass was asked to summarize his "signature look" and replied "...I think it's classic, timeless and clean-cut. I even like to think that it looks 'American' as opposed to European...it's a lack of embellishment...simpler, with more emphasis on fabric and line...."

However, Blass does not limit his designs to simple, exquisitely cut clothes. Blass clothes are for the woman who delights in dressing up. For evening wear, he is known for gowns in luscious, clear-hued silks and satins as well as elaborately beaded and sequined outfits. Equally, his day wear has a subtle elegance, with his own sense of suave diplomacy expressed in every pleat and drape.

His stated love of simplicity does not preclude the image of the urban sophisticate, and Blass clothes have a cosmopolitan polish that is obviously influenced by his love of the glamour found in Hollywood movies. Interviewed by *W* in 1987, Blass stated "...Every Saturday afternoon with Garbo,

Dietrich, Lombard dressed to the nines...think of those clothes. Movies really gave me my background in fashion."

The clean lines of this jacket are embellished by stacking two patch pockets and adding contrasting buttons.

The classic sheath dress with a contrasting pleated drape exemplifies the Blass look of simple elegance.

Patch Pockets

T he challenge in making patch pockets is to turn them out in perfectly matched pairs and attach them with professional results. A variety of techniques will help you create your own handsome pockets.

Pocket Components

Patch pockets, usually made from self-fabric and applied to the outside of the garment, can be either lined or unlined, interfaced or not. As you make a pair of patch pockets, check carefully to be sure both pockets are exactly the same size and shape; attach them to the garment evenly where they look best on your figure. Pockets can beautifully accent expert craftsmanship or they can expose a poor construction job.

Interfacing enables you to obtain the custom look of a patch pocket. Interfacing provides added strength, reinforces the opening, and preserves the pocket line. Most pockets made in lightweight or loosely woven fabrics need to be interfaced. All pockets with buttonholes need the stability of an interfacing.

Adding a lining is the fastest way to sew perfect patch pockets every time. By lining the pocket to the edge, you can save time and skip steps. A pocket lining makes it easy to keep the edges even, the shape symmetrical and the size consistent. Most pocket linings are color-matched to the pocket itself; however, a contrasting lining may become an interesting design feature. You may self-line the pocket if the fashion fabric is lightweight and smooth enough.

You can achieve professional pocket linings in a variety of ways. We will present four of the best techniques. In Pocket One, used in couture sewing, the pocket and lining are constructed separately. In the other three methods, the lining and pocket are stitched right sides together and the pocket is turned right side out in one of several ways.

Pocket One: Couture Method

INTERFACING

A lightweight interfacing, compatible with your fashion fabric, is your best choice for controlling the shape and preventing bagging of your pocket. When using a sew-in interfacing, cut the interfacing piece the same size as the pocket, including the self-facing. As a guide, mark the $5/8$" (15 mm) seam allowance on the interfacing with a wheel and tracing paper. Pin interfacing to wrong side of pocket. Stitch $3/8$" (10 mm) from raw edge, using a loose tension set for machine basting, and a stitch length of 4 (6 stitches per inch). By hand, sew interfacing to pocket fabric invisibly along foldline between pocket and self-facing.

Interfacing
Mark $5/8$" (15 mm) seam allowance on the interfacing but stitch $3/8$" (10 mm) from raw edge. Trim interfacing close to stitching.

POCKET LINING

To make a lining pattern for this method, fold under a $5/8$" (15 mm) seam allowance along the upper edge of self-facing; fold again along the foldline at the upper edge. Place tracing paper over the pattern and outline the cutting lines at the sides and bottom of the pocket pattern; at the top, draw a line $5/8$" (15 mm) above the lower fold of the self-facing seam allowance.

Lining
Cut out lining from the newly formed pattern piece and stitch to upper edge of pocket self-facing. Press the seam towards the lining.

MAKING A POCKET TEMPLATE

A rigid paper template, cut to the exact size and shape of the finished pocket, streamlines the patch pocket pressing process. It saves time at the pressing stage and practically guarantees accurate and smooth curves.

To make a pocket template, place pocket pattern over a manila folder or cardboard, and trace the top foldline and the seamline $5/8''$ (15 mm) in from the bottom and side edges; cut out. To make a lining template, trace similarly, but trim the sides and bottom a scant $1/8''$ (3 mm) smaller than the pocket template. Label templates.

USING THE POCKET TEMPLATE

Place the template on the inside of the pocket, which is cupped from the gathering of the easestitching. Pull the easestitching to eliminate the fullness around the template curves. Press edges over template with tip of iron. Also press with a clapper to flatten bulk. Repeat the process with the lining template and lining. If fabric is bulky, trim away excess seam allowance.

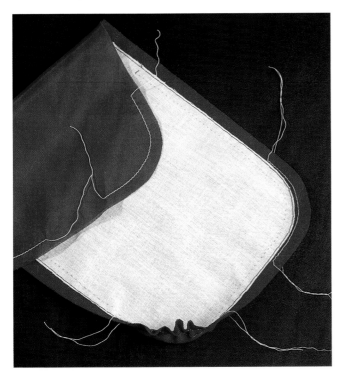

Easestitching Curves
Easestitch the rounded areas on both the pocket and the lining $1/4''$ (6 mm) from the raw edge. Carefully draw up the ease threads, cupping each rounded area.

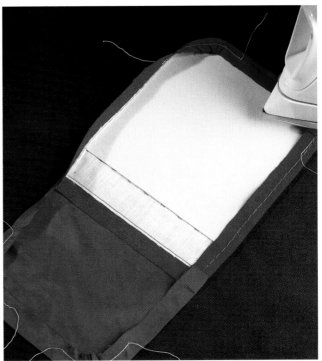

Using the Template
Use the template to shape the curved pocket edge. Press edge with tip of iron, steaming out extra fullness.

FINISHING

Turn the lining and self-facing to the inside along the foldline; pin together. The lining will be slightly smaller than pocket. Press along foldline. After you slipstitch the lining around the inside pocket edge and press, the pocket is ready for topstitching and application.

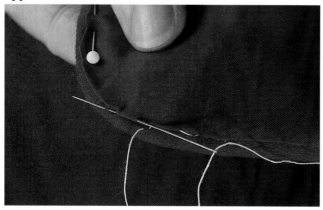

Slipstitching
Slipstitch the lining around the inside pocket edge.

Pocket Two: Faced Pocket with Lining

Using a pocket pattern that includes a self-facing, cut out a pocket and a lining. Interface if necessary. Finish the upper edge of the pocket self-facing in a method compatible with your fabric. Turn self-facing to outside along the foldline. Baste ends. Trim a scant $^1/_8$"

(3 mm) from the bottom and sides of lining piece; cut off section above foldline. To stabilize, stitch $^1/_4$" (6 mm) from the upper edge of the pocket lining.

Right sides together, center and pin lining to pocket, over self-facing. Use the pocket template to mark an accurate stitching line. Stitch, matching seam allowances and leaving upper edge open. Use smaller stitches when rounding the curves. Trim and notch the seam allowances along curve.

Turn pocket and lining right side out; slip the pocket template inside and press. Flip pocket self-facing over lining as shown; press again. Pocket is ready to be edgestitched in place.

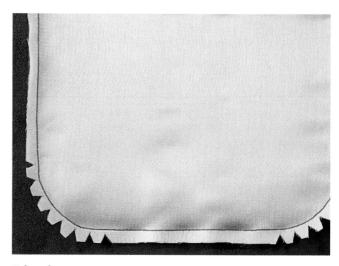

Trimming
Trim and notch the seam allowances along outer curves.

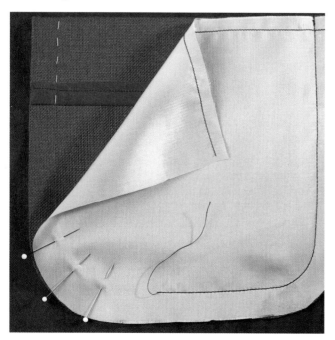

Stitching
Turn self-facing to inside and stitch remaining raw edges to lining.

Turning
Turn pocket right side out and press.

Pocket Three: Lined Entirely to All Edges

This method is appropriate for lofty and piled fabrics such as bouclé and velvet. Generally, this pocket would not be pressed crisp, and it would be sewn on by hand. A smooth, plain fabric with some body makes a better lining than a crepe, twill or drapy fabric.

Cut pocket from a pattern with $^5/_8$" (15 mm) seam allowances on all sides; cut lining from the pattern $^1/_8$" (3 mm) smaller on all sides. Apply an appropriate interfacing to the wrong side of the pocket. With right sides together and raw edges even, pin lining to pocket. Sew around edges from lining side, leaving an opening at the bottom. Use smaller stitches at curves and corners; make two stitches across points. Trim and notch seam allowances along the curves. Press around stitches, then turn pocket right side out. Nudge out corners and curves with a point turner. Steam pocket gently on the lining side, rolling outer seam slightly to the lining side. Close opening by slipstitching. Hand-sew invisibly to garment.

Pocket Four: Lined to Facing Edge

Unlike the previous pocket, this method allows you to stitch completely around the edges of the pocket, then turn it inside out through an opening between the lining and self-facing. This method works with all types of fabrics. Use a pocket pattern with a self-facing, and interface pocket appropriately.

With right sides together, stitch lining to facing edge of pocket, leaving a 2" to $2^1/_2$" (5 cm–6.5 cm) opening in the center of the stitching line. Press seam allowance toward lining. With right sides together, turn lining over pocket; match and pin raw edges together. Stitch bottom and side seams, using smaller stitches around curves. Trim and notch the seam allowances along curves.

Press to set stitches, then turn pocket right side out, pulling it gently through the opening. Using a point turner, nudge out corners and curves. Press pocket, rolling outer seam slightly to lining side. Slipstitch opening. Edgestitch or hand-sew pocket to garment.

Stitching
Stitch lining to pocket along all edges, leaving an opening along bottom edge. Trim and notch seam allowances at curves.

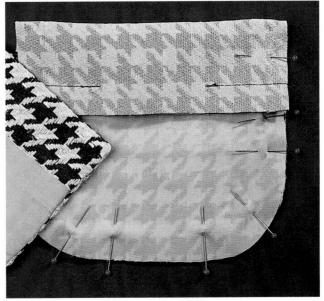

Pinning
Pin and stitch side and bottom edges of lining to pocket.

TIP FOR PREPARING A READY-TO-WEAR LINED POCKET

When preparing the pocket lining, trim a scant $^1/_8$" (3 mm) off the bottom and side edges. This will make the lining slightly smaller than the pocket so the seamed edges will automatically roll toward the inside, creating a neater finish. When pinning lining to pocket, keep raw edges of seam allowances matched.

POCKET WITH A BUTTONHOLE

As a design feature or for practicality, you may plan a vertical or horizontal buttonhole in a pocket. Apply interfacing between the pocket and lining. Make a sample buttonhole on a scrap of fabric, and indicate buttonhole markings on the pocket to assure that a well-made buttonhole will be correctly centered.

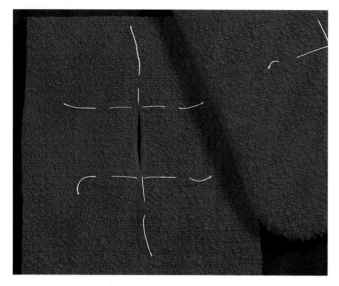

Pocket with Buttonhole
A buttonhole can be a design feature or a practical solution.

Pocket Placement

To mark pocket placement, tailor's tacks are always appropriate as they are visible on the right side of the garment and will not leave a permanent mark. Because your stitches go through both layers of fabric, your right and left pieces will be identical.

If fabric will not be damaged by a dressmaker's wheel and tracing paper, try marking on the wrong side of the fabric, then thread-trace markings to the right side. If you anticipate heavy use, reinforce the wrong side of the garment with interfacing under the upper fourth of the pocket area.

Attach patch pockets invisibly to the garment by hand-sewing from the wrong side. Create small diagonal stitches, using one leg of a cross-stitch along the sides and bottom of the pocket. Reinforce the sides near the opening area with a complete cross-stitch.

Another easy method for securing the pocket to the garment is to slipstitch it invisibly along the sides and bottom. To help hide stitches, "pinch-pin" pocket and garment just below the area to be stitched.

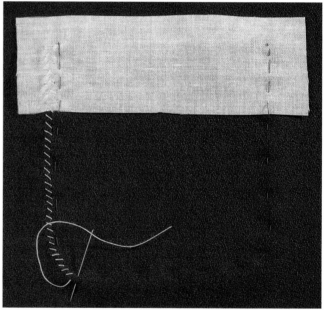

Method One: Attaching Pocket to Garment Back
Working on the inside, hand-stitch diagonally along the side and bottom pocket edges.

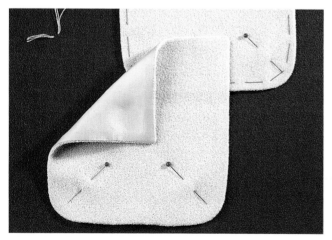

Hand-basting Pocket
Pin and baste pocket in position so symbols and markings match.

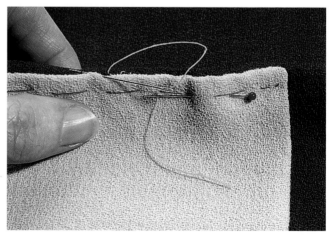

Method Two: Attaching Pocket to Garment
Working on the outside, slipstitch pocket edges to garment.

Attaching a Lining

Some designer finishing techniques are invisible to anyone except the wearer of the garment. They are "extra somethings," beyond the basic construction, that increase the comfort, convenience, fit and wearability of the garment.

A lining is one of those hidden components of fine, couture dressmaking that improves the finished effect of your garment. A lining helps retain the shape of your garment and gives it a more luxurious look and feel.

Cut your dress lining from the major garment pattern pieces. Construct and press it in the same manner as the garment, leaving appropriate seams open for closures.

Establish the dress hem length, fold and press along hemline, then baste close to pressed fold. Trim hem to an even width, using a serged edge or another finish appropriate to your fabric. Hem the dress, using a slipstitch about ¼" (6 mm) from the finished edge and easing out any fullness. Press.

Inside out, place the dress on a form or padded hanger to hang freely so you can move around the dress while working. Using pins, anchor the lining to the dress about 6" (7.5 cm) above the hem. Place pins at right angles every 2"–3" (5 cm–7.5 cm). Trim the lining even with the hemmed dress edge.

Finish the bottom edge of the lining in one of two ways. Hem the lining separately and allow it to hang free

and drape naturally, using French tacks at the seams to keep the lining from shifting. Or, slipstitch the lining to the dress hem.

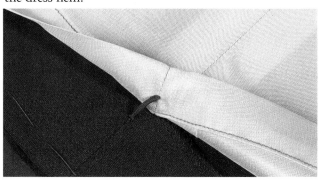

Hemming Lining and Garment Individually
Keeping the dress free as you work, turn up lining and press a hem 1" (25 mm) deep. Finish the raw edge by turning it under ¼" (6 mm) and pressing, creating a ¾" (20 mm) hem. If the hem edge is flared, add an ease thread ¼" (6 mm) from the raw edge. Edgestitch and press.

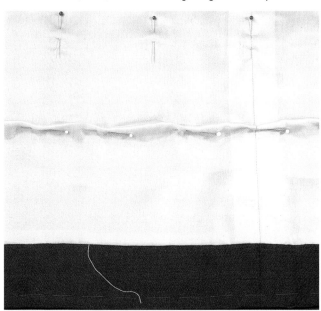

Slipstitching Lining to Garment
On the outside of the lining, pin a ¼" (6 mm)-wide tuck across the entire hem, below the pin line, placing pins parallel to the fold. Turn in the raw edge ¼" (6 mm), ease and pin to hem where it falls. Slipstitch lower edge of lining to dress hem; remove pins. Let the lining fall down over the hem, forming a soft fold. Gently steam into place. If there is a vent or opening, slipstitch remaining turned-in-edges of lining.

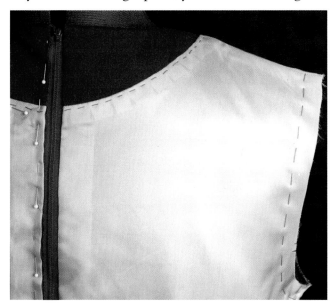

Attaching Lining to Dress
Slide the lining over the dress, with wrong sides together. Along the neck facing and armhole edges, baste the lining to the dress, treating the two layers as one. Turn under and slipstitch the lining edges to the zipper tape.

Belville Sassoon

Bellville
Sassoon

Karl Lagerfeld

Karl Lagerfeld

Belville Sassoon

CHAPTER 10

Designer Details

W hen you think of great couturier dressing, you probably think of gorgeous fabrics, dramatic silhouettes and hefty price tags. There's a reason for the latter; there's a great deal of behind-the-scenes handwork and inside garment construction that most people aren't aware of. As a home sewer, you can master these fantastic details.

The works of three designers show you the way. A Givenchy creation demonstrates how to add the requisite body to a structured silhouette. The fine tailoring of a Lagerfeld jacket offers a lesson in how to construct perfectly fitting sleeves. An opulent evening gown from David Sassoon of Bellville Sassoon shows how to build a strapless bodice to support an array of embellishments.

Givenchy

Givenchy

Hubert Givenchy

David Sassoon

Karl Lagerfeld

Givenchy

The Designer at Work

Since opening his own *haute couture* house in Paris in 1952, Hubert Givenchy has been patronized by discriminating women of all ages who seek simplicity, elegance and glamour.

As is the case with almost every renowned fashion designer, Givenchy spent years of apprenticeship with older masters. Givenchy was fortunate enough to have been able to learn in the great houses of Fath, Piguet, Lelong and Schiaparelli. When the time came for him to strike out on his own, economic constraints forced him to display every model of his premiere collection in inexpensive white cotton shirting. But his genius was recognized nonetheless, proving that excellent cut can triumph over mere material.

In 1955, Givenchy collaborated with Christóbal Balenciaga in the introduction of the chemise, or sack dress, which—in an era of cinched waists and full skirts—set the fashion world aflutter. This one design can be traced through the intervening years in many forms, from the mini dresses of the '60s to the chemise that Ralph Lauren redefined for the '80s.

Givenchy asserted his influence in the world of motion pictures, most notably dressing Audrey Hepburn in *Breakfast at Tiffany's.* Hepburn became one of his most devoted customers and wore his creations with more panache than any runway model could.

Givenchy's many years of study under the great designers taught him a respect for the finer points of expert dressmaking, which he honors in his creations, whether they are for his couturier customers or ready-to-wear.

The jacket silhouette is enhanced with contrasting overlays in an exquisite cut that require special underlining techniques.

Underlining

Underlining—a hidden but structurally important component—is one of the hallmarks of fine couture.

Designers' styles require fabrics to take many different shapes. They depend on either the fabric's natural ability to flare into a silhouette, or on hidden inner components that support the fabric in its desired shape. Underlining, when chosen and used correctly, will help achieve the designer's intended effect with relative ease. This concealed element helps garments retain their shape and wear longer. In underlining a garment, the designer uses only fabric that will comply with the drape of the style and will be attractive, comfortable, and smooth.

When choosing underlining, consider the type of care the fashion fabric requires. A washable fashion fabric necessitates a washable inner fabric. Use as much care in shrinking it as you do in shrinking the fashion fabric. Remember that even a steam iron can have different effects on the inner and outer fabrics, causing one to shrink more than the other or even shrink in a different direction.

Underlining (also known as backing) imparts a sculptured look to your garment. Cut it from the same pattern pieces as the garment fabric. Then baste and sew the underlining and fashion fabric together to act as one layer. When used for shaping, underlining gives the outer fabric the support necessary to hold a silhouette that otherwise could not have been achieved. It adds body, reduces wrinkling, and lengthens the life of your garment by protecting the outer fabric from wear.

An underlining will also facilitate marking and stitching your garment. First mark your underlining, pin it to the wrong side of your fashion fabric, and transfer necessary markings to the fabric. You can record light changes or adjustments on the clearly marked underlining without over-handling the fashion fabric.

Silk organza is a good choice for an underlining when you want to create interesting design details in a garment, such as cut-outs or lapped shapes, but you do not want extra bulk. Silk, rather than polyester organza, creases well when pressed, conceals seam allowances, and becomes an almost invisible edge without adding thickness. Silk organza is the chosen underlining fabric for this Givenchy jacket with lapped color blocks.

Machine-stitching the Underlining
Pin the underlining to the right side of the overlap piece, then stitch, clip and trim.

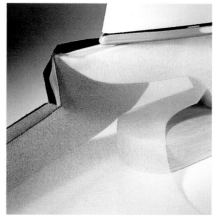

Press Seams and Underlining
Open the seams over a point presser, opening all the way to the corner. Turn underlining to the wrong side and press edge flat, favoring the outer side.

Lap Symbols, Edgestitch
On the outside, lap the finished edge over the seamline, matching symbols. Pin. Use an edgestitch foot along the finished edge.

Karl Lagerfeld

Lagerfeld mixes inventiveness and wearability, spicing the blend with a dash of wit in this fitted, below-hip jacket. The tapered two-piece sleeves have an elongated button vent.

The Designer at Work

Extravagant, exuberant, eclectic, Karl Lagerfeld always charms with his witty, *soignée* couture. Born in 1938, the designer spent his childhood north of Hamburg, Germany, in a country castle owned by his father, a wealthy dairy businessman.

This prolific, unpredictable, original designer is a master of his craft. In 1954, at age 15, he won an award for the best coat in the International Wool Secretariat design competition. Lagerfeld then became an assistant to Pierre Balmain, and after three years became restless and moved on to Jean Patou, with whom he worked for a year. After Patou, Lagerfeld began to make his mark by designing layered, floating silk crepe de Chine ready-to-wear ensembles for Chloé, an association that lasted for 18 years.

By 1983, Lagerfeld began his extraordinary career at the House of Chanel. His reign at Chanel invigorated the business, as he has mercilessly plundered Coco Chanel's historic contributions and served them up to the world with a new spin, displaying his own wit and style. Lagerfeld was not persuaded to sell under his own label until 1984, and his relentless imagination finds an outlet in designing furs for Fendi, as well as continuing to design for Chanel.

Set-in Sleeves

The tailored, two-piece set-in sleeve is considered the classic tailored sleeve that every sewer should master. You can learn how to prepare and insert this sleeve accurately and easily.

Checking the Pattern

Check the sleeve pattern for any necessary adjustments. Bending your arm slightly, measure your arm length from the shoulder bone, over the elbow, to the wrist bone. Compare your measurements with the pattern. Adjust length, then width. Generally the length is at the wristbone, and the width allows 2" (5 cm) of wearing ease in the upper arm.

Next, check the verbal description of your pattern to see if there is information about the type of shoulder: *slightly extended, extended* or *dropped.* These are technical terms explaining the extra design amount built into the shoulder length. See the illustration in Chapter 4 (page 45) to understand how the shoulders and sleeves of your particular jacket pattern should fit.

Constructing the Sleeve Cap

The trick in setting in a sleeve is to shape and mold the cap to fit smoothly over the shoulder before setting it into the armhole. Because the curved sleeve cap dimension is longer than the corresponding armhole, you will need to condense or reduce it. Make one row of gathering stitches next to the seamline, inside the seam allowance. Make another row 1/4" (6 mm) away, also in the seam allowance. Using a heavy thread in your bobbin will allow for stronger gathering threads which may be especially helpful in medium to heavyweight fabric. To provide a fit checkpoint for later use, sew a line of thread tracing across the sleeve cap—at notch level—on the crosswise grain.

To begin shaping the sleeve cap, hold bobbin threads and slide fabric along, easing fullness into the cap area. With right sides together and matching all markings, pin sleeve in jacket armhole, first matching seams and markings, then adjusting ease between pins. Fasten threads to hold gathers while proceeding. Hand-baste in place to prepare the jacket for a fitting.

Easing the Cap of a Two-piece Sleeve
Machine-stitch two rows of easestitches along sleeve cap seam allowance. Thread-trace along horizontal grain line.

Basting Sleeve in Place
Hand-baste sleeve cap to armhole.

FITTING THE CAP

Try on the jacket with the recommended shoulder pad and check the sleeve, using the thread tracing as a guide. The tracing should be parallel to the floor when you stand relaxed, with your arms comfortable and slightly forward. If the tracing slants, you will need to redistribute the sleeve cap ease to fit your arm shape and natural stance. Remove the necessary basting stitches and rotate the sleeve cap until the thread tracing is parallel to the floor. The sleeve cap should be free of creases, dimples and puckers.

When using a plaid or windowpane check (as shown), you may want to make a muslin sleeve at this stage. Draw several horizontal guidelines on the front of your muslin sleeve to indicate the placement of the lines/bars in your fabric design. Because of the ease across the sleeve cap, you cannot expect the back lines/bars to match. Transfer the guidelines from your muslin onto your pattern tissue and use them as a guide to cut out the sleeve from your fashion fabric.

Checking the Sleeve Fit
Make sure the thread tracing looks even and that the cap is free of puckers or wrinkles.

SHAPING THE CAP

Once you are pleased with the fit of the sleeve cap in the armhole, it is time to set the final shape. Before removing the basted sleeve from the jacket, provide yourself with new markings if you made adjustments in the sleeve cap and armhole. Tailor's tacks and thread basting line will work best as a temporary marking on your fabric. Remove the sleeve from the jacket and place sleeve cap over a press mitt or ham. Hold iron just over the fabric; steam well, allowing moisture to shrink out any fullness and mold the cap. Allow it to dry before proceeding to the next step.

Pressing Shape into the Sleeve Cap
Steam-press and shrink out excess fullness at seamline to shape the cap.

SEWING SLEEVE IN PLACE

Re-baste sleeve in armhole, check fit again with shoulder pad, and when you are pleased with the fit, machine-stitch sleeve in place. If you stitch with the sleeve side up, you have an opportunity to manipulate the fabric and control the eased-in fullness as you move along. Begin the stitching at the underarm area and return to it, overlapping a few stitches. Within the seam allowance, $1/4$" (6 mm) from the first row and between notches in the underarm, sew another row of stitches. Trim close to stitching only in this underarm area. Turn seam toward sleeve, and on a flat surface, press the seam with the tip of the iron on the inside of the armhole seam allowance, just to set the stitches.

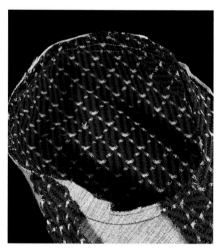

Sewing Sleeve in Place
Machine-stitch along seamline, adding an extra row of stitching along underarm curve. Trim close to this second line of stitching.

THE SLEEVE HEAD

A sleeve head supports the weight of the sleeve cap fabric and provides a graceful fall from the shoulder seam. It also buffers the sleeve seam and prevents it from "reading through" on the right side. For padding, cut a bias rectangle of lamb's wool, polyester fleece or flannel 3" (7.5 cm) wide and 4"–6" (10 cm–15 cm) long for each armhole. Make a 1" (25 mm) fold on one long edge. Centering the sleeve head, place the folded edge along the seamline with the wider side next to the sleeve and the raw edges inside the sleeve cap. Slightly stretch (ease) out the fullness along each side; slipstitch in place.

Attaching the Sleeve Head
Slipstitch the sleeve head along seamline, matching raw edges. Also shown are four options for sleeve-head fabric.

Shoulder Pads

On the pattern envelope, check the size of the shoulder pad recommended for the pattern. It will be the amount required to fill the space between your shoulders and the finished jacket. Sizes and shapes of shoulder pads may vary from year to year, dictating a particular silhouette which you may or may not like. But basic shoulder pads should not be omitted from a tailored jacket; they are essential for shaping and support in addition to a particular fashion trend. As a sure way of knowing how well your jacket will fit and flatter you, be sure to use the correct size shoulder pads when fitting your muslin.

After the sleeves and sleeve heads have been installed, try on the jacket for shoulder pad placement. Place center of pad along the shoulder seam, extending outer edge about $5/8$" (15 mm) beyond the armhole seam. Adjust pad for comfort, fit and a pleasing look. From the outside, pin pad along the shoulder seam. The edge of the pad should be at the cut edge of the sleeve; trim pad if necessary to conform.

Adding the Shoulder Pads
Sew pad to shoulder seam allowance. (Stitches do not need to go through the pad.) Loosely tack lower edge of pad in place.

EXTRA TAILORED TOUCHES FOR JACKETS

A jacket pattern can provide you with a great silhouette and flattering lines, but the shaping that highlights a tailored garment is dependent upon the proper use of interfacing. It must support the shape and withstand numerous wearings and cleanings without overwhelming the fabric's draping qualities. The interfacing also protects your fashion fabric from ridges that may form at seam allowances and darts during pressing and cleaning. Over the years, hair canvas has been the preferred interfacing in tailored wool jackets. It's available in a variety of weights which can be steamed and shaped along with your fashion fabric.

Often it's a good idea to reinforce the front shoulder area with an additional piece of hair canvas interfacing cut on the bias. To cut it, use the jacket front pattern piece as a guide; interfacing should extend from armhole to front edge including the shoulder and neckline edges, and end approximately two-thirds of the way down the armhole (bottom edge will be perpendicular to grainline). Trim off the seam allowances along the shoulder seam of the hair canvas. Catchstitch canvas along this seam, then baste edges of canvas along the armhole seam to give further support to the shoulder area.

In a similar manner, you may wish to stabilize the back shoulder area with a stay of cotton broadcloth or muslin.

Refer to a tailoring book for more information about other appropriate interfacings and additional construction procedures.

For a little more fine-tuning, designers often staystitch around the armhole. Easing in a slight amount of fullness at the lower front armhole will give a better fit to the bustline, while a slight amount of easing in the back will help shape the roundness of the shoulders. If the fabric you are working with is heavy or loosely woven, apply stay tape around the seamline of the armhole. This will prevent distortion through the life of the jacket.

Bellville Sassoon

The full-length overskirt, shirred bodice, and elegant taffeta fabric add drama to this dress.

The Designer at Work

Fresh from the Royal College of Art, a young Englishman, David Sassoon, joined fellow designer Belinda Bellville to found the firm Bellville Sassoon. Together they established a reputation with elegant clothing for a fashionable and famous clientele. Thirty years later, with Bellville retired, David Sassoon remains a bright talent in the world of fashion.

Sassoon has since teamed up with Lorcan Mullany, who designs under the label Bellville Sassoon—Lorcan Mullany. From their studio in Chelsea they create collections that show in London, Paris, Milan, New York, Munich and Dusseldorf. Their creations retail in Europe, Canada and the United States.

The name Bellville Sassoon is synonymous with glamorous evening wear. Princess Diana is probably the most famous customer; joining her are other members of the Royal Family, British nobility, European and American socialites and entertainment celebrities. Equaling the evening wear in splendor are Bellville Sassoon's sumptuous and romantic bridal gowns that show up at society weddings with regularity.

Sassoon successfully combines a flair for the dramatic and romantic with an eye for the lines and shapes that most enhance the female figure. His insistence on elaborate detailing and dressmaking lend his designs an aura of grand costumes for memorable occasions.

Lined Bodice with Boning

Creating elegant evening wear demands a mastery of techniques. Some are technical, such as those used in the inner construction. Others are creative, and go hand in hand with one's imagination, skill and glamorous embellishments.

Fitting Considerations

Fitting must receive high priority for off-the-shoulder looks. Since adjustments in this area are much more complicated than adjustments at the waist or hip, it is important to choose the pattern size that corresponds to your upper body measurements. Read "Personalizing the Gown" in Chapter 5 to find out how to ensure that the bodice will fit your figure. Construct a muslin bodice to test your adjusted pattern. When assessing your fit, remember to consider all the components of your garment: lining, underlining, boning, interfacing, interlining, fashion fabric and embellishments.

Bodice Components

The bodice of the strapless gown shown here requires three layers. The innermost layer is a lining reinforced with boning to provide the necessary sculpting and support for the other layers. The lining fabric is tightly woven, smooth and pliable. Choose a lining compatible with your pattern and fashion fabric. Sew a mildly stiff interfacing at the V in the neck edge of the bodice to form a casing for two short strips of boning. Attach longer boning pieces to front and back sides of the bodice lining to provide shape, stiffening, and the necessary support for the outside drape and embellishment. The lining itself acts as a facing to hide the inner structure and provide a comfortable and refined finish for such an elegant garment.

Prepare the middle layer or underbodice as an underlining and stabilizing unit for a shirred outer layer, using the same pattern pieces as the lining, but cutting it from underlining or the fashion fabric. This middle layer may also need an interfacing to support extensive embellishment on the outer bodice.

Once a foundation is prepared, fashion fabric can be draped, arranged, sculpted and embellished as inspired by the designer. The shirring of the outer draped layer adds texture and surface interest to the garment.

Consider the bodice of this Bellville Sassoon gown as an opportunity for you to create your own special effects through your choice of embellishments.

Applying the Boning

Boning strips are available in solid, coiled, or perforated form; all can be cut to a specific length. Solid boning comes in a casing which can be stitched to the lining. Coiled boning comes in a range of specific lengths with removable metal tips covering each end. Perforated boning can be stitched right to the garment without a casing or inserted in one you create; use $1/2"$ (13 mm) wide cotton bias tape or grosgrain ribbon.

Cut boning with casing the full length of the placement line, from the top edge to the bottom edge of the area to be reinforced. Slide casing down at each end to expose boning and cut off an amount equal to your seam allowance. You will need to treat the cut edge of boning in some way to prevent it from tearing and poking through the fabric next to it. Round-cut and smooth off edge of boning with a file and/or cover the cut tip with fabric.

Shirring the Bodice

A shirred bodice necessitates an outer "drape" larger than the finished bodice, which is gathered to fit the middle or underbodice layer. To gather a drape for an intended shirred section, hand- or machine-stitch in the designated seam allowances. Hand-sewing a line of gathering provides a soft, free-form effect. Machine-stitching two rows of gathering will produce a more controlled look; use polyester thread in the bobbin to prevent breakage under the stress of gathering.

Working from one end, hold both bobbin thread ends evenly as you slide and condense the fabric along them to the mid-point; repeat for the other end. Again, working in the seam allowances, pin the wrong side of the shirred drape to the right side of the underbodice. Baste raw edges together. Sew front and back pieces together at the sides.

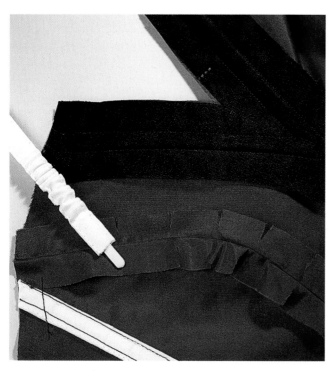

Applying Boning
Working on the wrong side, sew the fabric casing of the boning onto the placement line of the lining.

Shirring the Bodice
Draw up the gathering threads on the outer bodice drape.

Arranging and Sewing the Drape

To best distribute the drape and control the shirring, pin bodice to a dress form or a person wearing a leotard. Smooth each section so the bodice is taut and the drape is not straining or drooping. Manipulate the fabric with your fingers and pin all around between gathers and folds, holding fullness in place. The more pins you use, the more textured your surface will appear.

Remove bodice from dress form or model, and using a fine needle and matching silk thread, invisibly tack where each pin secures the drape.

Tacking Shirred Drape to Bodice
Tack the drape to the bodice middle layer at each pinned fold.

Applying Piping

In addition to defining the upper edge of the garment, piping helps prevent stretching. Staystitch the edge and measure it against your pattern to assure the dimension is the same as the pattern; adjust if needed. Easestitch a few inches from the side seam, near the dip at each front underarm section. Draw up ease-stitching to subtract $^1/_4$"–$^3/_8$" (6 mm–10 mm) which regulates the ease over the bust. Reinforce the inner corner with a series of small stitches leading up to it. Hand-baste piping to upper edge of garment, matching stitching lines. Backstitch when you reach an outer corner; clip seam allowance of piping. To create a defined corner that will not flatten out or pull, roll back excess piping at the corner, backstitch on the other side of the corner; continue basting. At the inner

corner, baste piping over reinforcement stitches and clip seam allowance as needed. Cut piping so it extends 1" beyond the inner corner.

Using a piping foot, machine-stitch piping with the needle moved so it just clears the groove in the foot. End stitching $^1/_2$" (13 mm) from the outer corner, change stitch length to .5 (20 stitches per inch), stitch to corner, pivot, check that piping is not caught in the seam allowance, and continue with small stitches for the next $^1/_2$" (13 mm); return to normal stitching. Stitch piping just to the point of the inner corner. Trim seam allowances except at an end near a closure; then trim cord out of seam allowance area.

Piping the Upper Bodice Edge
Machine-stitch piping to upper bodice edge along basting stitches using piping foot..

Facing the Upper Bodice Edge

Complete hand embellishment (see next two sections) before facing the piped edge. If using an appliqué, apply facing/lining before tacking motifs in place.

Place the right side of the garment over the right side of the lining. Pin, then hand-baste along the seamline; use small stitches near the corners, backstitch at the corners, turn and check that piping is not caught in seam allowance. Still using zipper foot, but moving the needle another degree away from center, sew closer to the piping than the previous row of stitches. Clip and grade all seams before turning right side out; press carefully on the faced side.

Adding a Trim

Creating an embellished design on a garment gives you a chance to express your own creativity. Strive for a pleasing effect that will enhance the character of your garment. Often contrasting elements are more effective than matching ones. Plan two to four compatible trims in your design. If the trims will be overlapped, there should be some similarity in their repeats. Some trims can be stretched, steamed and molded to conform to your design.

Determine the placement of your trim on the garment and mark with tailor's tacks or chalk. To support the area to be embellished, back with wool felt, then pin trim in place. Run several strands of 24" (61 cm) long thread through beeswax, sandwich them between strips of fabric and press with a hot iron. This will make the threads smooth, strong and tangle-free for hand sewing.

A couture method of finishing a braid-type trim is to backstitch the trim three times through all layers at the point where you wish the trim to end (without cutting trim close to backstitching). Unravel the trim beyond the backstitching and thread it through a carpet needle. Pull dismantled trim through to the underside of the garment and tack to secure. If trim is bulky, you may need to pull parts of the trim through separately.

Applying the Trim
Hand-sew trim, using a stab stitch in a zigzag pattern.

Bead Embellishment

There are many embellishment options for completing your design. Choose from a variety of beads, antique buttons, sequins, rhinestones, jewel stones, pearls and novelty adornments.

Added Embellishments
Here's the moment to suit your fancy and pull out all the stops, choosing from a dazzling array of beads and other embellishments .

Test your choices to make sure they will not shrink or discolor in the steaming or cleaning process. Which adornments you choose and where you place them will be part of the hands-on creative process. Strategically sprinkle them around and play with their positioning until you achieve a pleasing pattern. To prevent design distortion, sew the beads and adornments on from the center of the design and work out to the sides.

Sew beads on individually with a running stitch, or sew several beads or adornments together with a single stitch. Backstitch frequently during the course of your work. For lasting results, use beeswaxed, cotton-wrapped polyester thread. Metallic threads also give interesting effects. A size 10 beading needle works well most of the time; however, very small beads may require a finer needle.

Givenchy

Givenchy

Karl Lagerfeld

Karl Lagerfeld

*Beville
Sassoon*

Index

Acknowledgments

Project Designers and Samplemakers
Kathy Davis, Dort Johnson, Barbara Kelly, Kenneth D. King, Linda Lee, Sharon Ruddy, Marcy Tilton

Special thanks to the staff of Threadwear and The Sewing Workshop for their generous and expert support.

Step-by-Step Photography
Andy Cohen, Lawrence E. Cohen, Frank Kuo

Photographed at Studio One Productions

Additional Photography
Page 15: Courtesy of Ritter Cabinet Company; Page 75: Nathan Ham; Page 92: Studio One

The following are runway and/or ready-to-wear shots.

L = Left, C = Center, R = Right, B = Bottom, T = Top

Page	Designer
18TL, 18BL, 18C, 19	Donna Karan
28C, 28BR, 29T, 29BR	Calvin Klein
40, 41BR	Linda Allard
52, 53	Victor Costa
64, 65	Claude Montana
76, 77	Geoffrey Beene
88, 89, 92	Todd Oldham
100, 101	Bill Blass
110TL, 110TR, 110BR, 123BR	Bellville Sassoon
110BL, 110C, 111BR, 123BL, 123C	Karl Lagerfeld
111TR	Hubert Givenchy
111BC	David Sassoon
111TL, 111BL, 123TL, 123TR	Givenchy

Pattern Listing

The following is a list of the patterns featured in this book.

L = Left, C = Center, R = Right, B = Bottom, T = Top

Page	Pattern Style	Designer
2	Vogue 1308	Bill Blass
6	Vogue 1070/1071	Calvin Klein
7	Vogue 1256	Todd Oldham
8TL	Vogue 1187	Donna Karan
8TC	Butterick 3256	Linda Allard for Ellen Tracy
8TR	Vogue 1257	DKNY
8BL	Vogue 2596	Bellville Sassoon
8BCL	Vogue 1054	DKNY
8BCR	Vogue 1270	Calvin Klein
8BR	Vogue 1236	Calvin Klein
10	Vogue 1208	Karl Lagerfeld
18BR	Vogue 1293	Donna Karan
20	Vogue 1165	Donna Karan
21	Vogue 1293	Donna Karan
28BL	Vogue 2850	Calvin Klein
29BL	Vogue 1070/1071	Calvin Klein
30	Vogue 1202	Calvin Klein
31	Vogue 1070/1071	Calvin Klein
34	Vogue 2850	Calvin Klein
41	Butterick 6709	Linda Allard for Ellen Tracy
42, 43	Butterick 3080	Linda Allard for Ellen Tracy
44	Butterick 6709	Linda Allard for Ellen Tracy
54, 55	Vogue 2618	Victor Costa
66	Vogue 1251	State of Claude Montana
67	Vogue 1252	State of Claude Montana
74	Vogue 1253	State of Claude Montana
78	Vogue 1259	Geoffrey Beene
79, 80	Vogue 1203	Geoffrey Beene
90	Vogue 1256	Todd Oldham
91	Vogue 2873	Todd Oldham
96	Vogue 1256	Todd Oldham
102, 103T	Vogue 1308	Bill Blass
103B	Vogue 2767	Bill Blass
112	Vogue 1082	Givenchy
114	Vogue 1208	Karl Lagerfeld
118, 119	Vogue 2805	Bellville Sassoon

Due to changes beyond our control, over time, these patterns may no longer be available. When this happens, call 1-800-766-3619 to order the pattern. Limited stock is kept for one year from the date the pattern is discontinued. For further information, call Consumer Services, 1-800-766-2670. To order your free pattern, fill in the coupon on page 127.

FREE

VOGUE ᴼᴿ BUTTERICK PATTERN

To thank you for buying <u>Vogue & Butterick's Designer Sewing Techniques</u>, we would like to send you a FREE Vogue or Butterick pattern of your choice.

Just fill in the coupon below and mail it to:

Vogue/Butterick Pattern Service
P.O. Box 549
Altoona, PA 16603

Canada:
Vogue/Butterick Pattern Service
P.O. Box 4001 Station A
Toronto, Ontario M5W 1H9

Offer open only to residents of the U.S. and Canada.

Vogue & Butterick FREE PATTERN OFFER
(Include $1.00 for postage and handling)

Please send me the following pattern:

❑ Vogue pattern   ❑ Butterick pattern

Pattern #_____ Size_____
                                        (If applicable)

Name _____
                        please print
Address _____

City _____ State _____ Zip _____

Allow 2-4 weeks for delivery. Offer good for all Vogue and Butterick Patterns except 1001 and 1002.

SS/DES

ISBN: 0-671-88878-1
$17.00

For more sewing projects, look for the other Vogue & Butterick books featured on the Sewing Today television series:

ISBN: 0-671-88873-0
$17.00

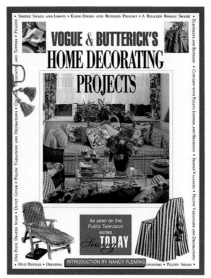

ISBN: 0-671-88877-3
$17.00